Bright

SEEING SUPERSTARS,
LISTENING TO THEIR WORLDS,
AND MOVING OUT OF THE WAY

Praise for *Bright*

"*Bright* is a breath of fresh air. Many books have been written on the topic of brightness, giftedness, and talent, but Alan brings something unique to the conversation. A pioneer in his field, Alan brings a deep and sensitive insight into the worlds of bright children. A rare breed himself, he has the gift of anticipating the very next question that the reader has. It is as though he is reading your mind in the best possible way! He expertly handles the subject matter with humour, confidence, pragmatism, and compassion, with a writing style that is accessible, intelligent, and mature. As the parent of an exceptionally gifted child, and director of a school for gifted children, I consider *Bright* essential reading for any parent or teacher of bright children."

— **Dr Kirsten Baulch** MBBS FRACGP GCBA. Parent of a gifted child. Director of Extension Education.
www.ExtensionEducation.com.au

★★★★★

"Alan presents profound concepts with a simplicity and clarity that makes powerful and passionate ideas available to readers of all ages and backgrounds. *Bright* encourages parents and families to realise they have the capacity to become 'experts' and to make a real difference in the lives of their highly able children. This is a book I will read more than once!".

— **Dr Gail Byrne** MAPS MCEDP MACE. Educational Psychologist. Exceptional Children.
www.ExceptionalChildren.com.au

★★★★★

"*Bright* is a delight. This book is filled with useful information and practical strategies for parents and teachers who want to nurture talents and help children develop their abilities."
— **Michele Juratowitch.** Counsellor. Director of Clearing Skies. www.ClearingSkies.com.au

★★★★★

"*Bright* is a 'must-read' for every parent, teacher, or manager who interacts with bright people every day. Alan Thompson writes from his own experience as a bright person and combines extensive research with powerful practical tips. Authentic, passionate, engaging, and innovative—this book will touch your heart and inspire you to the core. Enjoy every page!".
— **Otto Siegel** MCC MEd. Founder and CEO of Genius Coaching USA. www.GeniusCoaching.com

★★★★★

"What a delight to experience a book that moves beyond the metric of high IQ towards empowering bright kids to find their passion, persist in the face of adversity, and achieve true joy in life. Alan Thompson's latest work titled *Bright* inspires parents and educators to nurture emotionally secure, resilient, confident gifted children who have the skills to find a path towards brilliance."
— **Karen King** MAPS. Counselling Psychologist. Brainbox Psychology Clinic. www.BrainboxClinic.com.au

★★★★★

"In his book, Alan Thompson reminds us to trust bright learners: to trust that high ability is like an underground stream that will always find its outlet, if we get out of its way and don't block its path. He reminds us that adults do not have to push children to

achieve, but simply follow their passions. We must not commit soul murder by doubting bright children with the question, 'Who do you think you are?' but must listen to and honour who they are. And he reminds us that play = learning."
— **Dr Louise Porter.** Child Psychologist.

★★★★★

"What can I say... I LOVED THE BOOK! *Bright* is a refreshing and informative book that captures the reader's attention from start to finish. Alan Thompson uses a blend of research and anecdotal information to create a substantive, yet easy to read, text. His use of powerful coaching questions throughout the book provides an opportunity for insight and answers."
— **Jodi Sleeper-Triplett** MCC SCAC BCC. CEO and Founder, JST Coaching & Training. Author of *Empowering Youth with ADHD*. www.JSTCoaching.com

★★★★★

"Alan D. Thompson uses wide ranging and eclectic sources in this clear and coherent primer for parents of gifted children. Using a readily accessible format he leads us through the identification, potential issues, nurturing mental strength, self-control, minimising self-sabotage and how to actively support our gifted children. It's not about 'doing it for them', it's about 'letting them do it'. The joy inherent in every page of this book is infectious and invigorating. *Bright* infuses its readers with confidence and enthusiasm, giving loads of practical advice, resources to investigate, and a set of new viewpoints. An invaluable read for anyone who has taken that first step in identification. Set them up... and step back!".
— **Lise Harper.** Educator. Treasurer for Mensa New Zealand.

★★★★★

"In this well-researched and easy-to-read book Alan addresses key issues that bright children struggle with like self-sabotage and lack of focus. The book uses examples to develop reader awareness of the challenges that both parents and their bright children face, and it builds to a stunning conclusion with 100 practical advice tips. While this book is excellent for parents of bright children it should also be read by bright adults!".
— **Diane Spencer-Scarr.** *Managed Evolution through Digital Engagement.* www.Spencer-Scarr.com

★★★★★

"As a teacher who places the utmost importance on the social and emotional wellbeing of the young people I teach, and as a musician with a passionate belief in the power of music, *Bright* was a heartening read. Although bright and brilliant children are the focus of this book the content is relevant to anyone who nurtures children, regardless of IQ."
— **Gillian Binks.** Special Education Teacher.

★★★★★

"I really love Alan's book, because in addition to helpful advice to parents, teachers, and bright children about how to let brightness flourish, it reminds us of the most important thing we all keep forgetting about: brightness is something to be celebrated!".
— **Marianna Rusche.** Psychologist. Mensa Germany.

★★★★★

"Parenting gifted children is hard and it is easy to focus on the negatives. Alan's book is refreshingly upbeat with a ton of practical advice for families of gifted children. Based on extensive research, this modern handbook is a handy reference for the day-to-day challenges we face."

— **Rebecca Evans.** Parent of a gifted child. Director of SWISH Education Australia. www.SwishEducation.edu.au

★★★★★

"A common sense approach to understanding giftedness—a topic that is often misunderstood by parents and teachers. More importantly, this book provides practical down-to-earth yet research-based ideas to maximise the potential of gifted children. It skips the technical jargon and yet summarises relevant research for everyone who wants to understand and support their gifted children and students more."

— **Delia Nicholas.** Parent of a gifted child and a registered and practising teacher.

★★★★★

"Thompson's excitement about the potential of young exceptional minds is infectious. You will marvel at the intellectual capacity of the young people he has worked with. You will reflect on bright people you have come across in your life and understand them just that little bit more. You will want the super bright to be given every chance to become their 'best selves', for their own good and for the good of us all. You will relax in the knowledge that this is entirely possible, the toolbox is right here in your hand. A must-read for teachers, parents, and anyone who wants practical, real life guidance in giving bright individuals the environment and space to thrive."

— **Natalie Peterson.** Parent. Business Manager for Totally Sound.

★★★★★

"Such an amazing book! It is a real treasure-trove of valuable experiences, expertise, and knowledge. If only we'd had it earlier! Now I can feel the real value of play for bright children

and the importance of bringing playfulness, support, acceptance, and optimism to life!".
— **Sonja Kitak.** Parent of bright twins. Teacher. Coach.

★★★★★

"I really loved the book... the format encouraged learning, inquisition, and curiosity (the very definition of good teaching and learning). I wanted to shout about how important it was—in this terrifying, rapidly changing world—to have a voice like Alan's encouraging and celebrating the brilliant minds (and their parents!) that will save us. But I don't know that I can find a precise and succinct way of expressing this. So, if I was to say anything it is the following: 'My only regret in reading this book was that I allowed my busy life to get in the way of my reading it earlier!' ".
— **Neville Talbot.** Parent. Music educator. Musician. Conductor. Manager Tetrafide Percussion. Artistic Director Albany Sinfonia.

★★★★★

"Each child has a unique innate claim to live their best life. *Bright* by Alan D. Thompson vividly illuminates what it means to have a bright child, how to uncover your child's brilliance, and how to nurture bright children to give their best gifts to the world. An amazing read with many practical applications for everyday life."
— **Travis Bergsgaard.** Parent. Writer. Entrepreneur.
www.TravisEric.com

Other books by this author:

Welcome: Stories to wake up to!
Best: A practical guide to living your best life

Bright

SEEING SUPERSTARS,
LISTENING TO THEIR WORLDS,
AND MOVING OUT OF THE WAY

ALAN D. THOMPSON

Bright: Seeing superstars, listening to their worlds, and moving out of the way

First Edition, June 2016 (v2)

Copyright © 2016 by Alan D. Thompson

"Diagram of male and female" by Jon Lomberg. Copyright © 1977. All rights reserved. www.jonlomberg.com

"Dabrowski's five sensitivities" by Jessie Cat. Copyright © 2016. All rights reserved. www.pencilpaws.fi

Some chapters based on previous articles by Alan D. Thompson. *Pancakes and honey: Realising personal responsibility for high performance in bright children* (2016), *Resilience: In a bouncy ball* (2016), *Children with superpowers: The magic of advanced brains* (2015), *Confidence: More compelling than smarts* (2015), *Facing the right direction: Schools are not the problem... or the solution!* (2015), *Illumination: Edited readings for perspective* (2015), *Insights, Takeaways, and Bottom Lines from the 2015 International Conference on Giftedness and Talent Development in Brisbane* (2015), *Is my child gifted?* (2015), *Practice, practice, practice: Promoting passionate persistence* (2015), *Bright to brilliant* (2014). Copyright © 2014–2016. All rights reserved.

All rights reserved. No part of this book may be reproduced or copied in any form without written permission from the publisher.

All trademarks mentioned in the text are the property of their respective owners. This book is independent of any product, vendor, company, or person mentioned in this book. No product, company, or person mentioned or quoted in this book has in any way, neither explicitly nor implicitly endorsed, authorised, or sponsored this book.

ISBN-13: 978-1-5116-8464-4
ISBN-10: 1-5116-8464-X

Cover design by Lincoln Justus

Edited by Jessie Cat (Pencil Paws Consulting)

Printed by CreateSpace, An Amazon.com Company
Available from Amazon.com and other book stores
Available on Kindle and other devices

For further information, visit:
LifeArchitect.com.au

This is for you.

Contents

Foreword by Brian Castles-Onion 15
Acknowledgments 19
Introduction 25

Part 1: Growing up bright 33
What brightness looks like 34
Traits of brightness 43
The world is getting smarter 57
The source of brightness 68
Embracing boredom 75
Behavioural issues 83

Part 2: Ingredients for high performance 89
Seen and heard 92
Persistence 98
Resilience 110
Confidence 120
Play 134
Playing full out 145
Moving out of the way 153
Personalised learning 160

Teachers	175
Music	182
Personal power	191
Mentors	200
Technology	206
Coaching	212

Part 3: Tips for raising brilliance 225

Epilogue	241
Other acknowledgments	243
About the author	245
What Alan is up to	247
Next steps	249

Foreword
by Brian Castles-Onion

Right at the "coalface" of brilliance, Australian icon Brian Castles-Onion both works with high performers and is a high performer himself. Whether conducting for megastars like Placido Domingo, José Carreras, Dame Kiri Te Kanawa, or for a young international rising star, Brian has a colourful and playful way of being. He has taught at The Juilliard School of Music in New York and worked at New York's Metropolitan Opera. He is also a regular pianist and presenter on ABC television's Play School.

Recently, whilst sitting for my umpteenth portrait, the artist was attempting to engage me in a casual conversation to inspire her on-canvas representation of my personality. I am open and honest about most things in life—except my age. That subject came around quite quickly and, when I refused to admit an exact figure or year of birth, she asked, "How old would you like to be?". That was far more suitable. Being the eternal Peter Pan, I responded with: "Seven... but I loved being four."

It was an easy question to answer because those formative years are when one's mind knows no bounds. The world has yet to be discovered and every quest is achievable. When I was that age, my quest was to learn to play the piano. My parents—my father descended from a long line of coal miners, and my mother a dressmaker—had no idea what sparked my interest in music. They didn't expect it to be more than a passing phase, but I had a determination, a dream, that wasn't going away. All these years later, I'm still up there doing it, and the passion remains.

I've remained in touch with my inner child, and this has allowed me to maintain a career in music over several decades. The Peter Pan in me keeps on seeking the sparkle: that intangible thing that connects me directly to each member of the audience. I get to stand on the Maestro's podium surrounded by incredibly talented musicians in the orchestra pit, live my emotional life through the singers on stage, joke and gossip with the stage managers, mechanics and backstage staff, and be mentally transported by the music of the great composers.

Part of what keeps me connected to my inner child is working with and around children. On a long-running children's television programme in Australia I spoke to my young audience through music in many forms and styles—but always simple and fun. On one episode, two of the show's stars—a teddy bear named Big Ted and a doll named Jemima, both dressed in Ancient Egyptian finery for this scene—seamlessly segued Verdi's *Grand March* into *Walk Like an Egyptian*. I loved it—as did the children.

With a few on-screen appearances as "Brian", I have been recognised by my small fans on buses and trains, as well as in the Sydney Opera House! During a long run of *The Pirates Of Penzance*, children would frequently be seated in the front row, just a few inches behind the conductor's podium. As I'd take my entrance bow I'd hear, "There's Brian!" whispered excitedly to a parent. At interval I'd chat with the children, let them hold the baton and ask their thoughts on Act One. I'd gain new perspectives and new appreciations as they shared their impressions.

When an opera includes a children's chorus, I have sometimes been their Chorus Master. I am always amazed by the children's eagerness to absorb a foreign language, along with difficult music—and perform it at the highest level. It's not them "showing off". It's a hunger to experience everything available in life. There really is nothing more rewarding than embracing your passions, and sharing them with the world. It's an addiction.

We are all Peter Pan. It's just that some of us are permitted—encouraged—to follow through with our dreams, reveal our brilliance, and continue being superstars.

Brian Castles-Onion
February 2016
Sydney, Australia

Acknowledgments

In 1977, two spacecraft were launched into space by NASA: Voyager 1 and Voyager 2. Currently about 20 billion kilometres from Earth (even further as you're reading this, since they travel at 61 000 kilometres per hour!), they are the farthest man-made objects from our planet.

On board each of these probes is a time capsule. Its aim is to give extraterrestrials a story of the world of humans on Earth. Called the "Voyager Golden Records", they contain 55 greetings in many languages, a wide variety of music (including music from the Australian Aborigines), and 116 photographic images.

Of these 116 images, one is firmly embedded in my memory.

"Image number 32" is a silhouette of a man and a woman. In the black and white cross-section, it is clearly visible that the woman has a child in her womb. The parents have a technical note against each of them which says "20y"—twenty years old.

Carl Sagan's principal artist Jon Lomberg has very

kindly allowed us to use that artwork here.

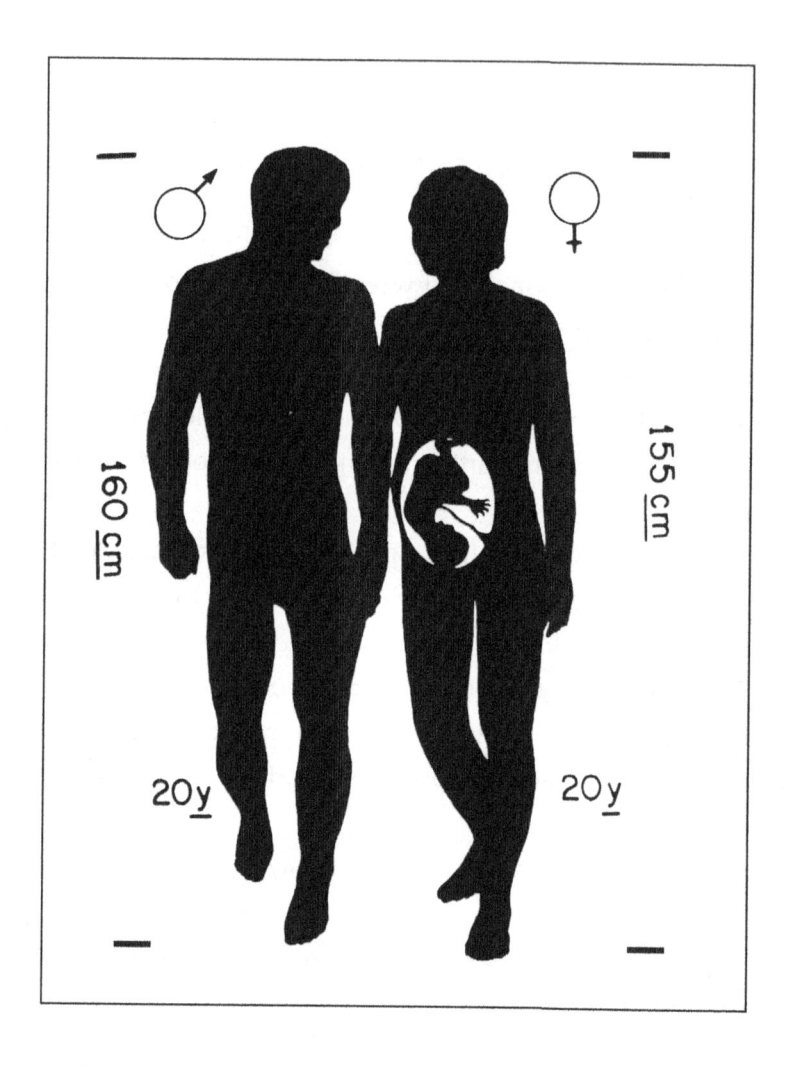

Of course, humans are physically capable of having children before the age of 20. But as a symbolic age of raising a child—one which we're comfortable telling the rest of the universe about—this number struck me for some reason.

Legally, in most countries the age of 20 is only two years away from being regarded as a "child".

So, as an adult, how are we expected to learn about raising a child—let alone a bright child capable of transforming the world? And what is the most important factor in supporting brightness?

Dr Greg Baer, an American author known for his concept of "real love", writes very directly about the role of parents:

> *Golfers, baseball players, lawyers, musicians, and so on all learn their crafts. And yet somehow we believe that when two people bring a child into the world, they are magically given the ability to love and teach that child. We prove our belief in this "parental magic" with the amount of attention we put into parental education. More training is required to get a fishing license than to be a parent. In high school and college, we teach algebra, history, and economics, but parenting is all but ignored. Then when we do a lousy job of loving our children, we're surprised. We shouldn't be. Loving children doesn't come automatically; it's something we learn to do, just as we*

> *learn anything else: we need to be taught, we make mistakes, and with instruction and practice we get better at it.*

The parents I've worked with over the years have been a shining example of power, courage, determination, and *devotion.*

Perhaps more than the media would give them credit for, these parents are the real champions in advocating for, supporting, and opening space for our high performers—our superstars!

I've devoured many of the books on brightness, giftedness, and peak performance. They usually start with a bleak definition of intelligence, veering off into testing and curves and probabilities and diagnoses. Sometimes these are mixed with "case studies", like some sort of bizarre science experiment.

But your child isn't a science experiment, and neither are you.

So, to you—parents, educators, and professionals—**thank you!**

For your unwavering commitment to your self. Being the supporter of a bright child can be like being thrown into a new life, one you didn't ask for. Seeing superstars, listening to their worlds, and moving out of the way is *simple,* but not *easy.* It takes an extraordinary person to be able to support and accept brightness while allowing the child to be self-driven. And all while they learn difficult—but valuable—lessons in life.

For your belief in, and attention to, your child. Bright children are amazing. They can certainly be demanding. Your continued belief and attention to their needs, to what is most important to them from moment to moment, is paramount to their continued confidence and success, something which they take with them into adulthood.

For giving your child whatever they are asking for.

Bringing out the best in bright children, supporting them and opening space for brilliance, is the most important job in the world.

For championing brightness.

Advocating on behalf of your child is an endless job. Thank you for allowing children to be heard and understood, and letting them know they are responsible for their own lives and brilliance.

For believing in the life-changing power of personal development—at any age.

Personal development isn't a luxury. It is the foundation of every single high performer on our planet. And the earlier this way of being can be accessed—and consciously worked with—the more effective our world becomes.

For deepening your own understanding of what it means to be brilliant.

It's exhilarating to be part of the continuing progress happening all the time. Parents, educators, professionals, and bright children themselves are all involved and responsible for this evolution.

For taking on one of the most challenging, emotionally exhausting, satisfying, enlivening, and important roles in the world.

Parenting of any kind can be a thankless role, and even more so when raising a bright child. The challenge of seeing superstars and listening to their worlds cannot be understated. And neither can the importance of doing so.

Thank you for being you.

Introduction

I am sometimes asked how I got into coaching high performers (with a focus on helping bright families reveal their brilliance). My life, like yours, has been filled with many twists and turns. For whatever role "luck" has to play, I do consider myself very lucky for having the background that I've had, and for the path I'm now on.

Philanthropist William Clement Stone talked about a process called "inspirational dissatisfaction". It happened to the creator of Netflix, who was sick of paying overdue fees at Blockbuster. It happened to the inventor of the telegraph (and joint developer of Morse Code), after he received a letter informing him of his wife's death—far too late.

For me, this process of inspirational dissatisfaction also started far too late (or perhaps right on time). It was my first job out of university, and the requirements were strict. The company only accepted the "top 1%" of consultants, something I thought would exclude me. Following a battery of psychometric testing, the CEO pulled me aside, and told me to take further testing. So

I did. At the age of 20.

What would have been possible had I known earlier? If I'd been given opportunities to explore myself, and the world? New languages, different courses, bolder directions.

And what would have been possible had I been offered coaching at a young age, perhaps at 10 or 11? Based on my experience, maybe I could encourage the parents of young people to have their children tested earlier and give them the encouragement and support that they deserve.

This feeling, this process of inspirational dissatisfaction, has driven my work with high performers in many industries. I feel I've been making up for lost time. In the 10 years between 2002 and 2012, I explored high performers in the world of strategy for Fortune 500 corporations, and at the intersection of creative and technical for the live events/performing arts arena. While the "corporate" side didn't do much for me, the live events world opened my eyes to the aliveness that comes through revealing—and realising completely—personal passion.

After five years on the road with creative organisations like Opera Australia, Red Bull GmbH, and Andrew Lloyd Webber's Really Useful Group, I found a unique base and a deeper peripheral passion: life, and the concept of coaching brilliance.

The idea of designing life, architecting life, is

something I have always loved. From my first foray into coaching (for myself) back in the early 2000s, to dressing room conversations with some of the world's rising stars, revealing brilliance and uncovering insights is always exciting and powerful.

A stickler for professional standards and sustainable methods (and as a recovering scientist), I sought out training resources and research findings with the most accomplished coaches and leaders on the planet. Through several innovative methodologies from around the world, I've discovered an incredible and distinctive process for hearing your child's brilliance, and revealing that brilliance for them and your family.

Some writers write to hear themselves talk. Of course, most of the literature available for bright families is heavy with PhDs, MEds, and old people in grey pant suits. Interestingly, many of them sound tired and angry; maybe from fighting the system for too long. Their papers are littered with graphs, bell curves, and clinical numbers.

The content is rich in theory and statistics, but often lacking in humanness. They are almost always light in "lightness".

This book changes all that.

Written *for you*, it covers what you need to know, rather than what is available in the millions of dry science journal articles (feel free to browse them at your leisure—they make great bedtime reading!).

Although I understand the science, and I've read a lot of the research, *most of the theory is meaningless* unless it is used with and applied to children in real life. It's not possible to graph your child's "passion for counting absolutely everything including nutritional information on food packaging", or their "motivation to learn to read the newspaper at the age of two". Those things are tangible, words don't do them justice. Comic book artist and creator of *Calvin and Hobbes* Bill Watterson puts it like this:

> *That's the whole problem with science. You've got a bunch of empiricists trying to describe things of unimaginable wonder.*

A handful of the questions in this book are extremely personal. Others dive deeply into the ocean of parents' and educators' "need to know" questions. They come from real people—my own clients, members of high IQ (intelligence quotient) societies, curious parents, interested educators—and they all combine a common thirst for more knowledge, more solutions, more results.

I have changed the names of all coaching clients (adults and children) appearing in this book. Some of them are composites based on conversations of coaching sessions. I have also edited and consolidated some questions for readability, and removed the questioners' names.

My responses have a solid foundation of research and "best practice"—a product of my training as a scientist. They also leverage my time spent working directly with high performers for more than 15 years. Of course, I've also intertwined my experiences from the 18 years I spent as a bright child. But, just as in my first two books, there is an aspect of the words written on the page that have come *through me*.

I haven't quite worked out where these come from. Experience? Or a more universal expression of support and acceptance?

I encourage you to examine the concepts here. Compare them with your own experience. Some of them seem universal, perhaps even basic. Some may prompt a response in you. That's a good thing!

The format of this book is designed for different learning styles, with an integration of both science-based research, and practical applications. Each section—each question—includes:

- A frequently asked question.
- A distilled answer.
- A detailed and expanded answer.
- Further questions for both you and your child.

- External resources (including videos, articles, and books) that you can search for to bind everything together.

You'll notice that I've taken a simple approach in uncovering the world of brightness. Research, yes. And stories. Real life.

No reference to medical dictionaries, no long-winded white papers that should have been kept as blank white papers, and no meaninglessly detailed percentages, line graphs, or extrapolations.

I don't think they belong in this conversation. Famous billionaire Warren Buffett identified this many years ago:

> *There is a great desire of the priesthood [in this case, academics] to teach what they know vs. what you need. If you know the bible in four languages, your ego won't allow you to teach the true essentials, which might be 'follow the 10 commandments'.*

This book could be summed up in just a paragraph:

> *Well done on raising your bright child, on your interest in and commitment to their continued development. A bright child*

> *needs ongoing love and support. Their valuable contribution will change the world.*

Actually, a paragraph would be too long. I wouldn't write at all. I would listen to you.

I've started many of my seminars with the following quote. It is from one of the founders of coaching, Bill Cumming:

> *Raising children is more important than any other leadership role on the planet… The way we're operating with one another needs to shift; it's not about the doing-ness… focus on intentions.*

Your work—as a parent, educator, or professional—is vastly more far-reaching than just "raising a child". There is a reason I've jumped into coaching for bright families and high performers rather than executives. This is where the magic happens. This is where the groundwork is laid. This is where leaders are created. Not in the boardroom, but in the classroom, home, and neighbourhood.

You only need to remember two things about supporting a bright child. They are the same two things needed for every human being on this planet—including you. And they are not so much about *doing* as they are about *being*.

1. Give your child absolute support and acceptance.
2. Show your child that they are powerful enough to create something important.

Finally, I'm not offering you any advice in this book. Rather, I'm giving you some universal truths about working with high performers, and some reminders for helping uncover brilliance.

But, as a gifted and high performance coach, I can't provide you with any wisdom you don't already have. My job is to listen and highlight your own strengths.

Listen to the ingredients and truths here, and you'll find that anything is possible for you, your bright child, and for the world. As you digest these pages, remember that despite the challenges and complexities involved in accessing a more advanced world—the world of brilliance—you've got it already. You are immensely powerful.

Alan D. Thompson
January 2016
Perth, Western Australia

Part 1: Growing up bright

Q:

What does brightness look like?

A:

Unlike tallness, or attractiveness, or fitness, brightness is completely invisible. Expressing brightness is as unique and varied as children themselves.

Bright children don't wear a sign around their neck saying "bright". They are the same as other children—they just have an advanced brain!

Do you remember your first day of primary school? Take a moment to think back to that time or the earliest days at school you can recall. The vivid colours. The smell of crayons and carpets. The jostle and bustle of backpacks and lunch boxes. The glossy covers of new books. The sound of other children talking and giggling. The newness. The anticipation of discovering new and different worlds.

I love the idea of school as a microcosm of life. There are parallels to be drawn between nearly everything at school, and the big wide world encountered much later in our lives. School, more than home, sets the stage for the absolute diversity of planet Earth.

In my primary school, as much as anything else, I remember the other students. I was brought up in Western Australia in the 1980s and 1990s, where primary school was for children between the ages of six and 12 (grades one through seven). But I saw reflections of the rest of the world, the foundations, in that first year.

Or maybe it was the first week. Sitting down to lunch with the other students, I went to open my drink bottle and noticed that the top had been tightened too much for my little fingers. I tried again, harder this time. Then I wrapped part of my shirt around it. Still it wouldn't budge. I had a solution: someone stronger than me. One of my new friends, Tim, was noticeably bigger than me. I asked him to open my drink bottle, and he did.

Perhaps because of his strength and height, Tim became one of the best basketball players in the school.

There were other children like Tim; children who had talents that were apparent.

Amber was absolutely stunning. Even in primary school, she was in demand as a model.

Melissa was well-built. She was particularly talented at quite a few sports events, especially throwing. Her shot-put and discus throws were always top of the class. She went on to represent Australia in the Commonwealth Games.

All these children had visible strengths. You could tell just by looking at them that something was different, that there was something to be encouraged.

But what about the smart ones? Intelligence, unlike beauty or strength, isn't something that can be seen. Yet, more than any other, the bright individuals that have existed since the dawn of time have created the world we live in today.

British writer Aldous Huxley has an intense declaration of the output of bright children:

> *Perhaps men of genius are the only true men. In all the history of the race there have been only a few thousand real men. And*

> *the rest of us—what are we? Teachable animals. Without the help of the real man, we should have found out almost nothing at all. Almost all the ideas with which we are familiar could never have occurred to minds like ours. Plant the seeds there and they will grow; but our minds could never spontaneously have generated them.*

My physiotherapist's son, Michael, has a problem. It's one that his dad knows all too well. Michael has pronounced issues with his neck and spine, such that his neck (and chin) stick out awkwardly. After years of diagnosing patients, his dad knows exactly the reason for this as well: "Michael is very tall. Taller than any of his peers. His neck problems stem from years of stooping down to talk to his friends."

Tall people (and their challenges and advantages) are visible. We can see them. They are over-represented in the sports and modelling industries. They are catered to by the medical industry. They stand out in daily life.

Bright people don't have any of that visibility. We can see height; we can't see an abstract concept like *mental processing*. Devastatingly, we can't see the often self-imposed issues of hiding brilliance. Like Michael experienced, there are costs and benefits of stooping down to the level of peers.

There is no direct comparison between the gift of intelligence and any other gift in life (tallness, beauty, charisma). The extraordinary ability of brightness means that people with this gift really are given more. More capacity, more to process, more to experience, and more to express.

So, how do we measure brightness? The first workable IQ scale came to us from Alfred Binet in the early 1900s. Using some fairly dry maths, parents are usually exposed to the scientific "IQ curve" as a way to visualise brightness. I'm not a huge fan of this, as it doesn't adequately show the distribution of brightness through the population.

So, I re-wrote it. Here is the IQ chart that I use to explain brightness. Please note that the labels at the top of the chart are suggestions only. They are based on several interpretations, including those given by Professor Miraca Gross, who in turn derived them from French Canadian psychologist Françoys Gagné's poorly delineated (but unfortunately, widely accepted) definitions. They are provided as an indicator only.

ALAN D. THOMPSON

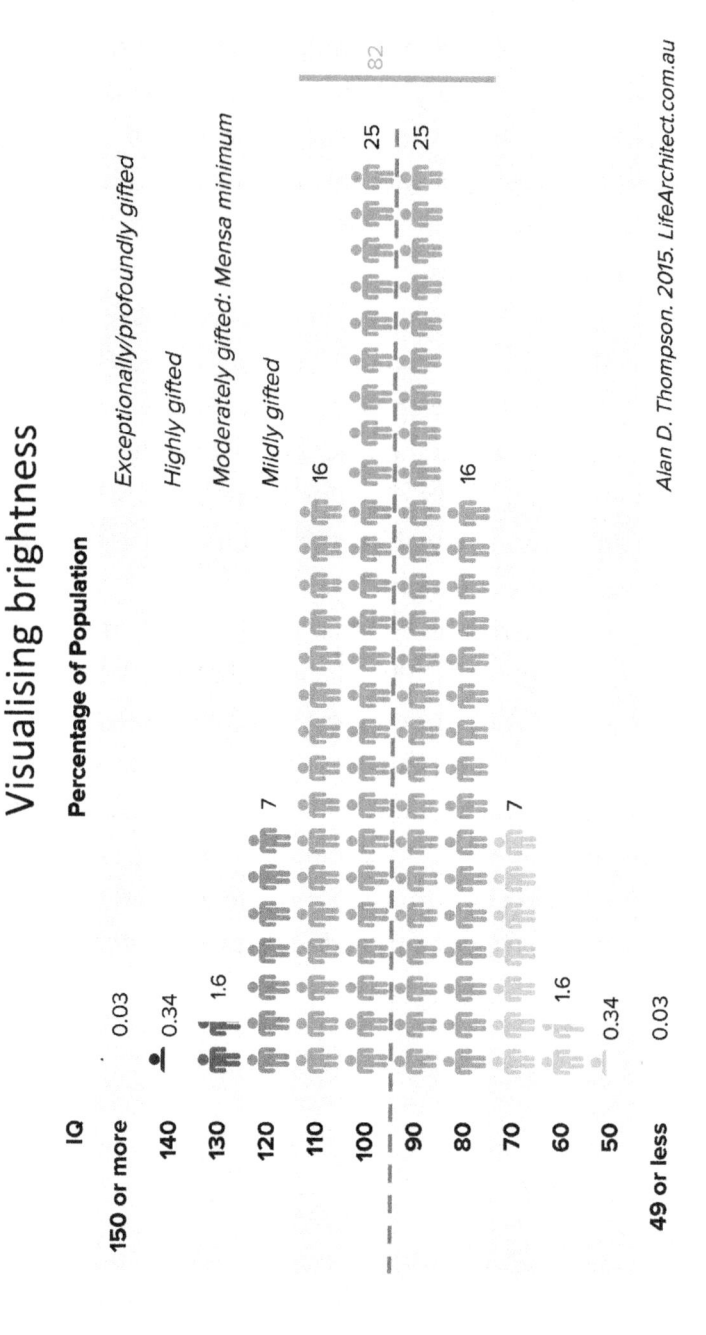

Visualising brightness
Percentage of Population

IQ	%
150 or more	0.03
140	0.34
130	1.6
120	7
110	16
100	25
90	25
80	16
70	7
60	1.6
50	0.34
49 or less	0.03

Exceptionally/profoundly gifted
Highly gifted
Moderately gifted: Mensa minimum
Mildly gifted

82

Alan D. Thompson. 2015. LifeArchitect.com.au

If you suspect that your child is somewhere near the top of this chart, the best first step is to have them tested.

Australia has some of the most outstanding psychologists available for testing your child's IQ. Obtain a recommendation for a trusted psychologist in your area who uses the standard tests: either the Stanford-Binet or the Wechsler. Both tests are accepted for joining societies like Mensa, as well as being recognised by most Australian schools.

Whether or not your child is gifted, do remember that they are unique, and that they have an innate claim to live their best life—to reveal their *brilliance*.

And, once you've found an answer to the question: "How bright is my child?" (or "How gifted is my child?"), get ready to move on to the more important question (covered in part 2 of this book): "Now, what are we going to do about it?".

Take it further

Questions for adults:
- What interests you most about brightness?
- How committed are you to exploring the world of brightness?
- If your child is able to reveal their own brightness, what would that mean to you?

Questions for children:
- What do you **think** about being bright?
- How do you **feel** about being bright?
- What would the world be like if everyone had the same brain?

Resources
- **Read:** Leta Stetter Hollingworth's free book *Children above 180 IQ (Stanford-Binet): Origin and development.*
- **Watch:** Iain McGilchrist's video *The Divided Brain.*

Q:

What are the traits of brightness?

A:

An advanced brain. That's it!

Of course, there are other traits associated with advanced brains, but they will vary greatly from child to child. These can include a deep thirst for new data, an intense curiosity, and an inspired sense of humour.

Several years ago, a journalist from a major newspaper conducted an interview with me regarding bright children. The interviewer was looking for some short, sharp sound bites; a handful of platitudes and generalities that she could use to put all bright children in a bucket...

I recall one of her questions: "What are the common traits or characteristics of brightness?".

I was silent. I was surprised at her question. To my mind, there was only one trait of brightness: an advanced brain. There is no standard set of characteristics for brightness—bright children are individuals. Would she have asked the same question of tallness?

Just as a child who is tall has the characteristics of *being tall* (above average height), a child who is bright has the characteristics of *being bright* (above average brain). Anything past that starts to get a bit more complicated. Traits and characteristics, things we think of as "innate", may actually be side effects of the *environment* the bright person finds themselves in. The *wrong* growth environment can bring about defensive behaviours. Imagine being permanently placed in a tribe that can't understand you.

Defensive behaviours can include tantrums, hiding/isolation, contrarianism/arguing and other coping habits that aren't innate traits. These can easily creep into adolescence and adulthood too, with things like impatience, boredom, cynicism, and intolerance for injustice showing up as children get older.

The problem, of course, is that brightness isn't visible in the same way as tallness (or attractiveness or physical strength).

So, how else would you identify brightness in your child—or indeed in any person—without an IQ test? The bright child's advanced brain leads to exceptional ways of seeing the world, and what scientists like to call "overexcitabilities". Although I'm not a big fan of the term, I believe that these are the closest we will ever get to shared characteristics. They were identified by Polish psychologist Kazimierz Dabrowski. Dabrowski was interested in gifted research, though his theory is not limited to the gifted. In fact, his original research was on groups of highly creative, artistic children from all walks of life. More recently, another psychologist, Michael Piechowski, collaborated with Dabrowski and applied these sensitivities to the gifted population. Several psychologists and educators have since added to research on the subject.

They don't all apply in the same way to every gifted child, but they are a great concept to help visualise and group sensitivities evident in the extraordinary brain:

1. Psychomotor: rapid speech, massive enthusiasm, intense movement.
2. Sensual: heightened sensory experiences, such

as with fabrics, fragrances, music.
3. Intellectual: intense curiosity, voracious reading, love of theory, concerns about ethics.
4. Imaginational: use of metaphors, detailed drawings, rich dreams.
5. Emotional: intense feelings, including sensitivity to the feelings of others.

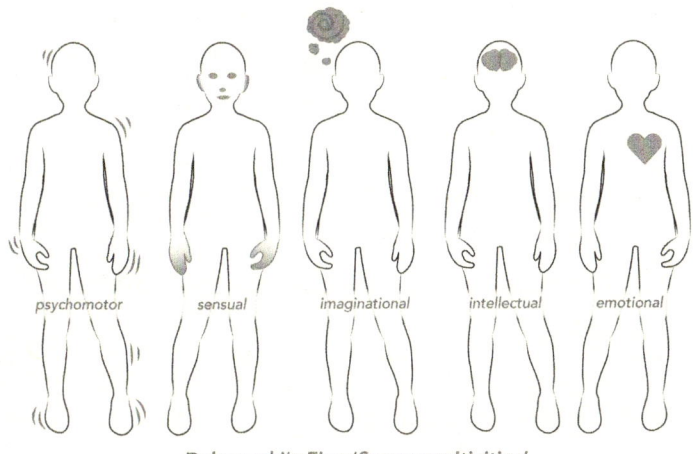

psychomotor   sensual   imaginational   intellectual   emotional

Dabrowski's Five 'Supersensitivities'

Pick a bunch of gushing adjectives: the advanced human brain is exhilarating, exciting, and immensely powerful. Much like Superman—faster than a speeding bullet and more powerful than a locomotive—some advanced brains have access to a whole array of superpowers. They make deep associations, sense vividly, process in parallel, memorise information, harness an extensive vocabulary, or apply combinations of these to daily life.

American husband-and-wife neurologists Brock and Fernette Eide have studied the advanced brain for decades. In their article *Brains on Fire: The Multimodality of Gifted Thinkers,* they comment on the physical characteristics of the advanced brain through functional brain magnetic resonance imaging (fMRI):

> *The first thing you notice when you look at the fMRIs of gifted groups is that it looks like a 'brain on fire.' Bright red blazes of high metabolic activity burst out all over the scan. Each red patch represents millions of microcombustion events in which glucose is metabolised to provide fuel for the working brain.*

What is the output of these advanced, hyper-focused, and hungry brains? What innate superpowers ("traits") can they possess—and take for granted—that seem extraordinary to the rest of the world? While the following superpowers don't apply to all bright children across the board (each child is, after all, unique), they give an overview of the possibilities inside each bright child. Here are just a few.

Vivid associations and sensing

One of my coaching clients was a gifted eight-year-old girl with diagnosed synaesthesia. Although this neurological condition is not a trait of giftedness, it is strongly linked with creativity and brightness. In this particular client, it showed up as an involuntary link between characters (numbers and letters) and colours. She would naturally "see" colours in response to each letter of the alphabet, or number. Many creative celebrities—from Australian actor Geoffrey Rush to American singer Lady Gaga—report applying this condition to their creative output as well.

These different sensory inputs include things others may not even consider: fragrance, colour, sound, images, words. The ability to make these advanced connections is a direct result of having an advanced brain. This facility to apply multiple inputs means that bright children are able to join the dots in vastly different ways. The "always-on" nature of the advanced brain—and its application to *every internal and external input*—means that bright children are at a distinct advantage when it comes to the sheer amount of information available to them.

Is it really any wonder that bright children process *everything* differently?

Parallel processing

At 10 years old, Australian boy Chris Otway had a tested mental age of a 22-year-old, and an IQ of 200. Chris was a child with a high-performing brain. Some of the superpowers that came with this brain included the ability to process tasks in the background—while his mind was resting or doing other things. In a discussion with Miraca Gross, Professor of Gifted Education at the University of NSW, Chris described his ability to "parallel process" problems. One example of this was his natural capacity to work on two complex maths problems at the same time. Miraca reported:

> *He seemed to be able to sense the point at which one set of predictions/speculations/calculations (Problem 1) was nearing the point of resolution. At that time he would put that problem on hold and bring Problem 2 to the forefront of his mind, aware that his subconscious mind was simultaneously working in parallel on Problem 1. When Problem 1 had attained resolution it would explode back into his conscious mind as an "aha!" moment which would bring the keenest intellectual and emotional pleasure. The solution would remain with Chris in detail and with complete clarity while he continued to work on Problem 2.*

One of the most striking things about the gifted population is the ongoing research helping with their advancement, and the advancement of average brains as well. Chris' ability to harness his subconscious—to "slow down" and let background processes do their job—is one that benefits a much larger population than just the top two percent.

Prodigious memory

At just three years old, Canadian girl Grace Hare recited 31 digits of pi in 18 seconds. Here's what that number looks like:

3.1415926535897932384626433832795

It runs in the family too: Grace's older sister Rose knew 63 digits of pi when she was five years old.

Along the same lines, Australian Mensan Daniel Kilov holds several records as a memory athlete. Mentored by fellow Australian Tansel Ali (who memorised the entire Sydney Yellow Pages in 24 days), Daniel is able to memorise huge amounts of information. From a shuffled deck of cards to 100 random digits to 115 abstract images, Daniel is able to hold vast sequences of information in his head.

Despite its unpopular reputation, rote learning and memorisation is an incredibly important facet of performance. It is a required foundation for deeper learning and understanding.

Even at very young ages, prodigious memory is evident. Australian Professor Brian Start found that in a standard mixed ability classroom environment, bright children could memorise information 12 times faster than the slowest student.

Applied to complex information processing (higher order thinking), bright children were four times faster than the slowest student.

Relevant data filtering

Whether it's grasping the intricacies of physics or the subtle beauty in music, bright children pick things up quickly. Faster than a speeding bullet, the advanced brain rapidly searches for patterns and connections, while retaining a deep understanding of useful information.

One of the reasons that this rapid processing is so efficient is because of the brain's ability to filter out the *noise* from the *signal*. American software engineering manager Michael "Rands" Lopp calls the advanced brain "an annoyingly efficient relevancy engine". Constantly scanning its environment for data to process and things to solve, it is adept at focusing—and discarding anything it deems irrelevant to the current task.

Extensive vocabulary

When he was seven years old, Greek boy Ioannis Ikonomou had already learnt English and German on top of his native tongue. By the time he was in high-school, he had added Italian, Russian, Arabic, East African Swahili, and Turkish. Now an adult, he is fluent in 32 languages including Latin and Sanskrit. He also understands that he is human: "I am not a machine. I do not speak languages perfectly. I have a Greek accent!".

One of the common items across gifted checklists is having an extensive vocabulary. Coupled with a firm grasp of language (including the use of metaphors), this superpower is visible across the spectrum of bright children.

Applied power

Bright children have access to a bunch of innate superpowers. But superpowers are only useful if they are used. All of this raw power needs to be harnessed and applied directly. Those bright individuals that have uncovered their capabilities—and recognised themselves fully—are the ones that will be able to bring their best selves to the world.

This decade, and through the 2020s, 2030s, and 2040s, the output of bright children is exploding. Looking at the creative and technological domain, 14-year-old American boy Zach Cmiel designed and developed 12 iOS games and apps currently available in the Apple Store.

At a deeper level of contribution, 11-year-old American boy Peyton Robertson connected the dots between his own talents and gaps in the outside world.

After flooding killed more than 200 people during Hurricane Sandy in 2012, Peyton created a new type of sandbag out of polymer. "Science is all around us. Ideas for new inventions come from my everyday life experiences. When my sisters were learning to ride a bike, I designed retractable training wheels with handle bar controls. After playing at an out-of-state golf tournament on a cold day, I designed a golf ball warmer to preserve its temperature and performance in colder environments."

More powerful than a locomotive

Having access to these extraordinary superpowers as part of the advanced brain is exciting. Even more exciting is the huge capacity for creating, which exists in each bright child. It is becoming increasingly important to provide the most appropriate resources for these children (and adults).

Affording bright children the opportunity to apply these superpowers in an ideal growth environment enables them to flourish.

Giving them unconditional support in exploring their capabilities—and with a meaningful understanding of their own needs, values, and strengths—empowers them to believe in themselves.

Listening to them as they realise their own capacity promotes deep confidence in the way they live their lives.

Allowing them to understand the difference between *memorising data* and *contributing to the planet* encourages bright children to bring their best selves to the world.

Take it further

Questions for adults
- What is your superpower?
- What do you see as your child's biggest advantage?
- How do you help your child use their advanced brain?

Questions for children
- If you could have any superpower, which superpower would you choose?
- How do you have a superpower already—and what does it look like?
- What things can you do that are easy for you?

Resources
- **Read:** Brock Eide and Fernette Eide's article *Brains on Fire: The Multimodality of Gifted Thinkers.*
- **Read:** Michael "Rands" Lopp's article *The Nerd Handbook.*
- **Watch:** Daniel Kilov's video *The art of memory.*

Q:

My child seems so bright. Is the world getting smarter?

A:

The world is getting smarter and smarter. Indeed, the new average is brightness.

Each year, each decade, each generation builds on the previous. Children today are brighter—they have better nutrition, more stimulation, and use different tools, in diverse environments.

In my 2013 book, *Best*, I described my exhilaration at walking into an Apple store, and being able to make a purchase with "no hands". The transaction was completed wirelessly, without a counter or a credit card machine.

Although, on the face of it, this incident was trivial, it highlighted huge advances in both *consuming* and *creating*.

First, bright children start their lives (and consistently continue) as consumers of data. They absorb information rapidly, digesting and processing the world around them.

Second, bright children quickly become creators. The brains behind the transactions in the Apple store would certainly have started life as bright children.

The world is getting smarter and smarter because our children are getting smarter and smarter. Both capacity (what a child is able to do) and performance depend on a combination of *genetics* and *environment*. And the environment—our world and the things in it—has been improving so significantly, that these performance increases are obvious. And hugely exhilarating!

Smarter, Earlier

It's easy to see the world getting smarter through the range of statistics available to us, including literacy rates across the developed world. Literacy rates have moved from around nine percent in 1475 through to a current peak of 99.7 percent (with variation depending on the region).

The age at which children—especially very bright children—begin reading has also been steadily decreasing. When applied to selected studies across the exceptionally gifted population (specifically, those with an IQ of more than 160), the average age for starting reading has dropped from around five years old in 1921 to under three years old in 1989.

Average Age Started Reading:
Gifted Children 1921–1989

Study start date	Original study	IQ >x	Number of children in original study	Average age started reading
1921	Genetic Studies of Genius (Prof Lewis Terman)	170	77	5 years, 1 month*
1925	Children above 180 IQ (Prof Leta Hollingworth)	180	12	3 years, 3 months*
1989	Exceptionally Gifted Children (Prof Miraca Gross)	160	15 (now 60)	2 years, 7 months
* Estimated from available data				

So we know that people can read, and that children are reading earlier. This may be exciting if we were moving from the Agrarian Revolution into the Industrial Revolution. But we've moved much, *much* further than that.

The processing that is going on behind the scenes in these advanced brains is a result of the continuing evolution of human beings, but more visibly, because of the broad and significant changes to the environment. This processing, and the measurement of this processing through IQ test scores, shows a clear "explosion" of brightness.

The Flynn Effect

Professor James Flynn (now a New Zealand local) is best known for his identification of IQ test scores increasing over time. It's not as clear cut as it seems though, and he illustrates this through a fictional story of archaeologists discovering and interpreting an increase in hand-eye coordination in shooting. Speaking at an international forum in 2013, Professor Flynn said:

> *...[in the year] 1865 [the archaeologists] found that in a minute, people had only put one bullet in the bullseye. And then they found, in 1898, that they'd put about five bullets in the bullseye in a minute. And then about 1918 they put a hundred bullets in the bullseye... How could these performances*

> have escalated to this enormous degree? Well we now know, of course, the answer... people had only muskets at the time of the Civil War and that they had repeating rifles at the time of the Spanish-American War, and then they had machine guns by the time of World War I. And, in other words, it was the equipment that was in the hands of the average soldier that was responsible, not greater keenness of eye or steadiness of hand.

Today, bright children are offered completely new, visceral experiences to develop and apply their smarts immediately. Beginning with computers, and moving into virtual reality and artificial intelligence, each version of technology in the modern world is strengthening learning, enhancing experience, and increasing brightness. In their book *The New Child: In search of smarter grown-ups,* Australian consultants Drs Patricia Edgar and Don Edgar say:

> The New Child's experience and facility with computers and other forms of digital technology are creating new brain connections, forging synapses and linkages that older adults have never had the opportunity to forge. So the way they see

the world, and the skills they have to deal with it, to operate in and on the world around them, may be markedly different from anything we have seen before.

These brain connections are happening as early as ever—mostly before the age of three. The world presented to bright children is rich and intense, in every medium: from the way people around them speak about concepts, to connected gadgets and smart phones, to advanced toys, to movies and media.

Never Mind Baby Einstein

Consider Australian television over the last few decades. Beginning perhaps with *Play School* (1966–present), the heart of several generations of childhood learning was born. The show was broadcast to children based on the work of several leading researchers, including Australian child psychologist Dr Rosemary Milne. The team behind the show included many other consultants, all involved in applying research to practice.

Australia's *Play School* preceded even that well-known "American institution" *Sesame Street* (1969–present). Supported by the US State Department of Education, *Sesame Street* was the first American program to be designed based on extensive formative research with both academics and children. Professor

Gerald S. Lesser conducted a series of seminars at Harvard University, incorporating educational pedagogy (teaching methods) and research into the original *Sesame Street* scripts. The show was and continues to be a leader in influencing other educational programs throughout the world.

More recently, Australia's *Lift Off* (1992–1995) was produced by Dr Patricia Edgar, and heavily influenced by Professor Howard Gardner's ideas. The Harvard professor's theory of multiple intelligences was used as an underlying foundation, integrating several layers of intellectual activity into the show's structure and narrative. It was also strongly linked with school curricula, being applied in parallel through Australian classrooms. In other words, national government policy recognised the benefits of schools partnering with researchers, giving children extended education through absorbing TV at home.

Today, given the steady audience decline of television in favour of online media, it is no surprise to learn of the decline of television programming quality as well. More modern early-childhood shows (including the BBC's *Teletubbies* and *In the Night Garden...*) lack the rigorous studies and applied research of earlier decades. However, children have just moved from absorbing information from one screen, to consuming *and* creating information on multiple, portable, integrated screens. Increasingly, this is even moving towards "screenless" digestion and management of information using some of the futuristic devices making their way into the learning environment.

Moving online

Just as there are substantive quality differences in television programming supporting bright children, there are also variances in all media. This is certainly apparent in the online world, where programming is completely unrestricted—anyone can create content.

Salman Khan's *Khan Academy* continues to lead the way in free online education. While his initial pedagogical content knowledge (PCK—basically the ability to teach concepts, rather than just understand them) has been questioned, the introduction of increased rigour and qualified educators has seen the program explode in popularity. Combined with online content from *Wikipedia,* several private learning applications, and the world's major universities, there is a universe of "sanitised learning" available online.

Even removing this sanitisation of "approved" education, when bright children interact with technology, they are learning—and not just learning to read.

Technology has brought well-rounded knowledge to bright children across the world. Children can now use technology to learn fine motor skills, visual and spatial skills, new forms of interpersonal and social skills, and even to develop a deeper understanding of themselves (including personal strengths and learning styles).

Onwards and upwards

All the doctors and professors mentioned in this chapter were (of course) children once. However, using Professor Flynn's formula of an increase of three IQ points per decade, and compared to the time these experts were children themselves, the average IQ for children being born today has increased by another 20 points. This is the same as the difference between "average" and "borderline gifted". In other words, the new average is brightness.

The world is getting exponentially smarter. Your bright child is part of that future, whether you're ready for it or not.

We can only imagine what is coming next.

Take it further

Questions for adults
- In what ways is the world getting better?
- How do you bring a positive attitude to your home?
- What do your responses to the world say about who you are?

Questions for children
- What is the best part about living on Earth this year?
- Who is the smartest person you know, and what makes them seem smart?
- What would you like to be creating when you grow up?

Resources
- **Read:** Chris Wayan's article *Prodigies' Oddities*.
- **Read:** Patricia Edgar and Don Edgar's book *The New Child: In search of smarter grown-ups*.
- **Watch:** James Flynn's video *Why our IQ levels are higher than our grandparents'*.

Q:

Where did my child get their brightness from?

A:

Brightness is part genetic, part environment.

Research shows that
brightness runs in the family.
But it is also a product of environment.
It's part nature (genetic),
part nurture (environment).

A fruit-seller. That's how it all started. Michael and his wife Luba (immigrants from Ukraine) lived in Connecticut, USA, and sold fruit.

There doesn't seem to be a record of their IQ, musical talent, or passion. Yet, you've definitely been exposed to the magic created by Michael and Luba's 10 children and even more grandchildren.

Beginning in the early 1930s, their first children—brothers Alfred, Lionel, and Emil—played a significant part in creating and defining the art of music in film and television. They were involved in leading musical roles for the themes and soundtracks of shows like *South Pacific* (1958), *M*A*S*H* (1972), *Batman* (1966–1968), and *Alien* (1979). Then, the children of Alfred, Lionel, and Emil took Hollywood by storm.

That moment before a movie starts—when the lights dim, the snare drum rolls begin, and the searchlights sweep the screen over the 20th Century Fox logo—that's Alfred's original composition right there. And his son, David, made the most recent recording of that introduction.

My first significant exposure to the Newman family happened while I was working as a sound designer for Opera Australia. One of the main functions of a sound designer is to recreate the same amplified sound at many venues around the world. To do this, tools like paper designs, electronic measurement, physical specification matching, and other scientific methods were used.

The one tool I came to rely on though, especially for "tuning" sound systems for Opera Australia and its prolific use of big orchestras, was pressing play on well-produced recordings that exemplified good sound. One such soundtrack was from Pixar's *Finding Nemo*. Composed and conducted by Thomas Newman (another of the grandchildren), the tracks had a dynamic quality that was unique. I could picture the fish swimming around; I could feel the different sections of the orchestra having a conversation with one other.

Many years later I worked with another Newman. Not Thomas this time, but David. It was at the Sydney Opera House again, and I was in a similar role. I was designing sound for both the 2600-seat concert hall, as well as each of the 94 orchestra members (all on headphones), and David himself.

It was this occasion that locked the Newman name into my mind. Using a tool designed by his father, Alfred, David conducted the orchestra in a live accompaniment of the 1961 film, *West Side Story*. And it was flawless.

The Newman family dynasty continues to produce musical scores for the latest blockbusters, including *Toy Story 3* (2010) and the latest James Bond movies: *Skyfall* (2012) and *Spectre* (2015).

Of course, there is a genetic component at play

here. But it is not solely genetics.

American psychologist Gary Marcus, from his book *The Birth of Mind*, writes:

> *The second biggest misconception people harbour about genetics: that it will be possible one day to determine, once and for all, whether nurture or nature is "more important". Genes are useless without an environment, and no organism could make any use of the environment at all if it were not for its genes.*

Keep in mind that children cannot be "hot-housed" to become bright (or brilliant). Indeed, there are many stories about the negative effects of attempting this. Professor Emeritus of Education and Psychology at Columbia University, Abraham Tannenbaum, once wrote:

> *Children with superior inner resources can fulfil their promise only if the nurturance they receive is "tailor-made" to meet their special needs; but without the requisite inner resources in a child, no amount (or type) of nurturance can make the difference between mediocrity and excellence.*

There is solid research on families carrying brightness all the way through the line. And in the case of the Newmans, through cousins and three generations. In her research on giftedness, American psychologist Linda Silverman found that IQ within families is usually very close: within five or 10 points for siblings, and within 10 points for parents and even grandparents.

This opens the way for testing all members of a family. If you notice brightness in one child, it is worth knowing just how far that reaches.

Take it further

Questions for adults
- Where do you see brightness in your family?
- How are you using your own brightness day to day?

Questions for children
- What would your life be like without your family?
- What is the most interesting thing about someone in your family?

Resources
- **Listen:** Thomas Newman's music in the movie *Finding Nemo*.
- **Read:** Marleen M. Quint's article *Lights! Camera! Music! The Newman Film Scoring Dynasty*.
- **Read:** Gary Marcus' book *The Birth of the Mind*.

Q:

How do I stop my child from getting bored?

A:

When bright children get bored, it is because they are not getting interesting information quickly enough. This is easy to remedy, but it is mainly the child's responsibility to learn and apply it to their own lives.

Bright children need to be living "up to speed" with their capacity. This can mean finding out more about their individual strengths, needs, and values. It also means removing any roadblocks and educating children about their options.

I was recently asked to teach a friend how to drive a manual car. For anyone who has tried to teach this, you'll know that it can be a challenging role (thanks Dad)! During the course of learning to use the pedals—especially the clutch—this friend managed to stall the car so many times that I lost count.

This stalling happens whenever the engine stops turning. After the engine has stalled, no combination of clutch, brakes, or accelerator alone will bring it back to life. Crying doesn't seem to help either. The ignition has to be fired again first, and the car will roar to life.

I notice this idea of "stalling" with bright children who are showing symptoms of boredom. They have stalled temporarily. They have switched off. They are waiting for that next spark to bring them to life.

Boredom is the opposite of aliveness. When bright children feel and act bored, it is because they are not "up to speed" with themselves; their lives aren't keeping up with their own vision for themselves. They need to catch up with themselves and their own advanced brains by living in alignment with their own power. Simple boredom—that is, when it's not a symptom of more serious and diagnosable depression—is often a great indicator that a bright child needs more of something.

This may be because they do not have access to enough information quickly enough. Perhaps they have not been provided with the right kinds of resources for their current interests. Or, it may be even deeper. Do they understand and realise their own values, strengths, and drive? Are they allowed to *be?*

For some bright children, boredom includes both physical and emotional discomfort. And humans don't like discomfort. One of the quickest remedies then, is to bypass this discomfort—any way they know how. Bypassing discomfort usually means that the child will withdraw and isolate themselves from the world. They can choose separation rather than giving of themselves completely. This lack of "aliveness" comes with its own set of challenges, including even more discomfort.

Another remedy is to become disruptive. This can be seen in bored children in standard old schools (SOS) all around the world.

The 1986 article *The Hacker Manifesto* is a well-known piece of text in the computing community. Written by an exceptionally bright young hacker, it highlights the frustration evident in that generation of bright children:

> *I'm smarter than most of the other kids, this crap they teach us bores me...*
> *...I'm in junior high or high school. I've listened to teachers explain for the fifteenth time how to reduce a fraction. I understand it.* "No, Ms Smith, I didn't show my work. I did it in my head..."

> *...we've been spoon-fed baby food at school when we hungered for steak... the bits of meat that you did let slip through were pre-chewed and tasteless.*
>
> *...The few that had something to teach found us willing pupils, but those few are like drops of water in the desert.*
>
> *We explore...*
>
> *We seek after knowledge...*

Bright children know when something is pointless or tedious, and will sometimes tell you this out loud, other times by hiding and becoming withdrawn. Of course, boredom doesn't just come from needing to complete schoolwork or other coerced tasks.

One of the benefits of being a bright child is their low boredom threshold. Bright children just don't accept boredom. They find a solution. They thrive on novelty and in-depth exploration.

An adult may let boredom have its way with them, becoming consumed by it. But bright children often step back to find some space from it. They find new and stimulating outlets, whether inside their vivid internal world, through obvious changes in their own behaviour (messages to those watching), or just plain old withdrawing.

Unlike their older counterparts, given the right environment and freedom, bright children will nearly always create their own solutions to boredom. They understand their personal power and responsibility in getting up to speed with their innate aliveness.

There is a beautiful pattern that I have noticed with embracing boredom:

1. Boredom. It begins of course, with that niggling feeling of "non-aliveness", whether due to a pointless activity, a tedious schedule, or a lack of resources.
2. Curiosity. Being able to push through this boredom begins with inquisitiveness. And this is a common trait of bright children. When they are allowed to explore their own curiosity, they get to move on to the next step.
3. Interest. Leaving boredom behind means lifting the corner of a new world, and having the freedom to dive right in.
4. Absorption. Once they have found an interest, bright children generally have an intense focus. Given the right resources, they are able to flourish again.

"The right resources" is a bit of a catch-all term, and is very much dependent on *who* your bright child is. Young children may just need simple resources to create their own new world. Do they need more engagement with sports? What about "walled garden" internet (age appropriate, of course)? A library card? More frequent access to their favourite hobbies? Time speaking with a mentor? Magazines targeted to their interests and age?

If dealt with effectively, boredom can be a lifesaver for bright children, leading them quickly to explore themselves further, and to reveal brilliance.

Parents and teachers play an important role here—but not by attempting to directly relieve a child's boredom through forced entertainment. It is about adopting a coach's mindset. Allow your child to find their own aliveness. Remove any roadblocks. Point the way. Have a conversation about the necessity of routine, but also every individual's power in bringing playfulness to life. And remember that boredom provides a huge opportunity for a child to apply crucial life skills including creative thinking, problem solving, and resourcefulness.

Bright children are going to spend the rest of their lives with themselves. Move out of the way. Allow them to identify and live their talents, strengths, and passions. Allow them to embrace and push through their boredom into aliveness.

Take it further

Questions for adults
- How excited do you feel about your life?
- How responsible do you feel about how your life turns out?
- How might your responses to these questions reflect your child's overall responsibility (and excitement) in their own life?

Questions for children
- What does your body feel like when you're bored?
- What would it feel like if life were exciting all the time?
- What is the best part about feeling bored?

Resources
- **Read:** Lucy Jo Palladino's book *Dreamers, Discoverers & Dynamos: How to Help the Child Who Is Bright, Bored and Having Problems in School* (formerly titled 'The Edison Trait').
- **Read:** Loyd Blankenship's essay *The Conscience of a Hacker* (also known as *The Hacker Manifesto*).

Q:

Why does my bright child have behavioural issues?

A:

Behavioural issues—while not an inherent sign of brightness—indicate that a child isn't feeling heard.

Minor behavioural issues (outside of diagnosed disorders) occur for many reasons. These can all stem from not feeling listened to.

Eight-year-old Gillian was having trouble at school. Her handwriting was sloppy, her test results were below average, she was talkative, known to "disrupt" the class, and she lacked focus.

Suspecting some sort of learning disorder, the teacher wrote to Gillian's mother requesting urgent intervention (due to bad handwriting and disrupting class). The teacher suggested that it might be more appropriate for Gillian to be in a school that catered to children with behavioural issues.

Her mother took Gillian to a psychologist for evaluation. The psychologist listened to Gillian's mother describe her "symptoms". He then tested Gillian, spoke gently with her, and then asked her to wait in his office while he spoke with her mother privately outside. As he left the room, he turned on the radio to keep Gillian entertained.

When the two adults were outside in the corridor, the psychologist took Gillian's mother over to a window with a view into the office. They watched silently. Gillian had stood up, moved into the middle of the room, and started rhythmically moving to the music on the radio. It was obvious that there was something natural occurring in her movements, and in her natural feel for the music.

The psychologist spoke to Gillian's mother: "Gillian isn't sick. She's a dancer. Take her to a dance school."

And she did. Gillian attended a dance school every

week. Then she joined a small ballet company. Later she joined the Royal Ballet Company. She appeared in theatre and films (including choreography for *The Muppet Show*). She worked for The Australian Ballet.

That girl grew up to become one of the most successful choreographers in the world, Dame Gillian Lynne.

She may be best known for her work as the creative brains and choreographer behind Andrew Lloyd Webber's *Cats* (1981).

This story has a personal connection to my life through my involvement in the *Cats* tour—now entering its 35th year and approaching $3 billion in ticket sales. As the head of sound for the Australian and Asian tours, I worked closely with Gillian's protégée, director Jo-Anne Robinson, to bring the vision of the show *Cats* to hundreds of thousands of people around the world. I also saw firsthand the enormous creativity and passion behind some of the most inspired and successful young people of our generation.

Of course, there are *real* behavioural issues as well—disorders that must be treated and diagnosed as such. But consider that brightness—a brain that processes more than usual—may include processing all sorts of things. Of course bright children may become frustrated and "act out" if they aren't able to bring this advanced processing into the world.

Take it further

Questions for adults
- What does your child get by misbehaving that keeps them coming back to it?
- How could you help them meet that need in a healthier way?
- What is your child's greatest strength?

Questions for children
- What does your parents' love mean to you?
- How does that make you feel?
- What is it that you want to say to your parents?

Resources
- **Watch:** Ken Robinson's video *Sir Ken Robinson tells the story of Gillian Lynne*.
- **Watch:** Gillian Lynne's video *Gillian Lynne rehearsing with Finola Hughes* (Cats *London 1981)*.

ALAN D. THOMPSON

Part 2:
Ingredients for high performance

There are standard ingredients for standard performance. First, there are the basic building blocks to consider. Breathing. Nutrition. Hydration. Adequate sleep. Sunshine. Exercise.

To go further than this—to cater to the advanced brain—requires the basics, plus a whole lot more.

Extraordinary brains need a lot of fuel to run. Grand master chess players can burn 7000 calories per day playing a single game of chess. For reference, the average adult burns only around 2000 calories a day, and that is through movement and physical exercise. The advanced brains of chess players are creating a 350 percent increase just by thinking. Stanford Professor Robert Sapolsky gave a presentation in which he explored the idea of burning these 7000 calories per day by brain power alone:

> *They are sitting there silently at a table. They make no eye contact; they're still, except every now and then one of them does nothing more taxing than lifting an arm and pushing a little piece of wood... They are going through 6 000 to 7 000 calories a day... and it's all with thought, and memories and emotions.*

And Professor Sapolsky is correct, it is not just thought. It is also memories, and the application of those memories to process input from the current moment. Even feelings and emotions are much more intense for bright children, because their broad awareness means that they are processing more data more rapidly. While your bright child processes things—all things—differently, humans are not computers. We are all emotional beings. Of the millions of pieces of data processed every second, the "feeling" part of this is what makes us human.

What else is necessary for a bright child to be *brilliant?*

Let's take a look at some of the core ingredients that are necessary in the lives of those who are ready to perform at their peak.

Q:

How can I recognise my bright child?

A:

Bright children are often *seen* for who they are.

Brilliant children are both *seen* and *heard* for who they are.

Seeing bright children, recognising their brightness, and reflecting back to them who they are, is the first ingredient of high performance.

At a very young age, Robert was told who he was. Born into a political family in South Australia, Robert was given the best of everything. When he was about 10 years old, his family moved to Perth, where he attended Perth Modern School and later, the University of Western Australia. Robert's mother would tell him that one day he would be the prime minister of Australia. At the age of 15, he was telling his friends and others around him the same thing. Robert James Lee "Bob" Hawke led Australia from 1983 to 1991, and holds the record as Labor's longest-serving Prime Minister.

Pablo was born into an artistic family in Spain. His first words were "piz, piz", Spanish slang for "pencil". He was drawing and painting at an expert level by the age of seven. His mother—wanting to support him to the highest level—said to him: "If you are a soldier, you will become a general. If you are a monk, you will become the Pope." Pablo Picasso became known as one of the greatest and most influential artists of the 20th century.

Leo was born into a football-loving family in Argentina. Despite having a growth hormone deficiency (making him shorter than others his own age), Leo showed early signs of high performance in football (soccer). Both his mother and his maternal grandmother supported him, taking him to his first training and matches from the age of four. They would tell him: "Hear me: you are going to be the best player in the world." A prolific goal scorer, Lionel "Leo" Messi is today widely regarded as the greatest football player in the world. Messi also holds the Guinness World Record for most professional goals scored in a calendar year: 86.

American violin instructor and gifted teacher Dorothy Delay had a saying about supporting this kind of brilliance:

Kids become what you tell them they are.

There is enough evidence of children moving from brightness to brilliance in the world; it's not just the three brief stories above. Without exception, I have noticed this trend with every high performer I have worked with or researched—hundreds of them.

For parents and teachers (though mostly parents due to the closeness and time spent together), this identification and verbalising of "what you say they are" happens whether it is intentional or not. In the examples above—and in the case of all high performers—parents and teachers have intentionally *seen* and *heard* the child's capabilities, and brought them to life through words.

Of course, this is only the beginning of high performance.

A bright child's sense of deserving comes from their very first environment. In fact, it begins around the same time they start to discover their sense of self as an infant.

As they grow up, they learn to treat themselves as others treat them. If their parents show them love, they feel good about themselves and their body. It goes further than just understanding their intrinsic value—they know what they can do, and they know who they can be.

Their level of deserving is not related to behaviour and actions.

Whether or not you've been raised in this blissful way, it's important to be aware of it, so that you can help create it with your own children.

I'll leave you with some final questions to consider:

What would you do if you woke up in the body of your childhood self? How would you get yourself more quickly to where you needed to go?

When you've thought about that, know that we can do the same thing for your child right now.

Take it further

Questions for adults
- What capabilities do you see in your child?
- What are you already saying to them?
- What are you committed to personally?

Questions for children
- Who would you like to be when you grow up?
- What will it take to get there?
- What if it takes longer?

Resources
- **Read (with your young child):** Nancy Tillman's book *On the Night You Were Born*.
- **Read:** a biography of a celebrity or eminent person in your child's favourite field.
- **Read:** a biography of a celebrity or eminent person in your own favourite field.

Q:

My child gives up easily. If something seems hard, they don't try. Why?

A:

Bright children are used to doing things easily; it's one of the best parts about having an advanced brain. When they come across a difficult or time-consuming task, it can be jarring.

The sooner bright children learn that persisting with a task is vital—even if they encounter setbacks—the better they will be in living their brilliance.

Resilience—adapting well in the face of adversity—is paramount to life. And a key factor of resilience is the quality of sticking to a task despite failures.

Depending on upbringing, a child has their personal course set by a combination of internal resources (including intelligence), modelling (parents and teachers), and environment (home and school). A fundamental aspect of their personal course is how willing they are to stick with a task. This concept of "persistence", while important, is not a very popular one. Persistence is the personal decision to press on with a goal—but not just because of a positive outcome, or even because the task itself is fun. Indeed, it is the moments when the task is proving *unsuccessful* that persistence is needed. American psychologist Martin Seligman (with Christopher Peterson) talks about persistence as choosing to press on with a project "in spite of obstacles, difficulties, or discouragement". Seligman also found that the quality of persistence (and self-control in sticking to a task) matters twice as much as IQ.

IQ + persistence

When high IQ is coupled with high persistence, our highest achievers thrive.

Bright children—those born with advanced brains—typically learn effortlessly. Their unique way of seeing and processing the world allows them to grasp concepts quickly and easily. Often, they become used to this way of accomplishing tasks, and of learning things.

The violin can be a fun instrument to learn while the child is succeeding, while the music is inspiring. Young astronomers can be endlessly fascinated by the stars, spending hours researching planets and systems. The ubiquitous obsession with dinosaurs can be a source of play, even while memorising their Latin names.

But what happens when children encounter a roadblock? And what can be done to encourage them to push through barriers that get in their way?

Bright children often have a minimal risk appetite outside of their own core talents and strengths. Relying on a history of excelling without much effort, many of them feel apprehensive about completing projects poorly, so it can be confronting to find something that doesn't come easily to them. Rather than appear to be "slow" or "wrong", they can be reluctant to even try starting new tasks.

Professor Miraca Gross explains:

> *Discovering that they are not the most mathematically gifted student in the school, that there are skills they have not yet developed, and that they may fail at a task two or three times before succeeding at it— and learning that these are experiences*

> common to the vast majority of the people they will encounter in life—can bring these students' self-perceptions closer to reality. Everyone has to learn that temporary failure—sometimes repeated—is a necessary step on the way to success. It is better for students, even the most gifted, to learn this in a supportive, encouraging school environment, and grouping gifted students together makes it much easier for teachers to present them with work that will require effort, persistence, and commitment.

Bright children, of course, eventually grow up to be bright adults. Bright children lacking task persistence usually grow up to be adults lacking task persistence. You don't have to look too far to find people who give up just before the point of succeeding; people who make an untimely decision to quit a particular project, course, or career because they don't feel that they have what it takes to succeed.

It may seem that some bright children at times aren't motivated by a specific action—examples include practising handwriting, cleaning up a room, or completing standard teacher-assigned work. Usually this means that the specific action, in this specific moment, presented in this specific way, is not satisfying to them. Lack of persistence doesn't suggest that the drive for learning has decreased, but that completing a specific action in a specific way does not meet the child's needs. Lack of persistence indicates a lack of relevance of a project to their current interest. When persistence is coupled with a child's passion—and a worthy challenge—children are able to tap into a rich personal source of confidence, accomplishment, and satisfaction. Even if the result is an "unsuccessful" project.

Practical applications

It is crucial to promote the quality of persistence to children from a young age. While it seems to be an innate function of giftedness, it needs to be nurtured to become a lifelong quality. Allowing children to discover their talents and strengths, and to work with those, is certainly valuable. Demonstrating the benefits of success and the necessity of deliberate practice helps children understand and realise the effort required to reach levels of mastery.

Both parents and teachers are incredibly well-positioned to provide individual and group support to bright children. (Although finding opportunities to model persistence to students is a tough ask in the classroom setting.)

Below are a number of practical examples for promoting persistence in bright children.

Nurture support and acceptance through extreme optimism in the home and classroom. Create a positive environment—both socially and emotionally—to allow children to feel safe and supported. When children are fully accepted and supported, they internalise this, speak to themselves more positively, and treat setbacks as fleeting rather than catastrophic.

Find out what your child's goals are. As a coach for bright families, most of my work is spent focusing on what children are good at. In fact, during every evaluation coaching session, I ask families two questions: one for the child, and one for the parent. I ask them to answer their question using their hands to build a Lego model (an *engaging* tool based on imagination and constructivism, rather than a passive tool). For the child, I ask: *What do you want to be when you grow up*? For the parents, I ask: *How do you want to use the rest of your life*? Goal-setting is a fundamental part of being alive.

Of course, children aren't expected to have a solid life purpose all mapped out. But they will usually have a current focus, obsession, and passion. Listen to their worlds. Keep personal and classroom goals visible. For teachers, even if these are "classroom-promoted" goals (like assignment due dates), they should be visible in front of the student as text or pictures.

Provide resources for children to learn about other people's goals—especially others like them. There is no shortage of inventors and celebrities facing adversity and triumphing. Famous basketballer Michael Jordan is a great role model for persistence. During his career, he averaged 11.5 missed shots every single game. When he retired, he'd racked up more failures than successes, having missed 12 345 shots during professional matches. In Australia, both Cyril Callister (the inventor of Vegemite) and Maggie Beer (popularising the modern adaptation of verjuice) persisted with no visible results for 15 *years* before their products even began to gain traction.

Provide children with a real challenge. We've all heard the story of the student who mistakes an "unsolvable" maths problem for homework, takes it home and solves it (both a true story, and a plot point in the film *Good Will Hunting*). Prominent persistence researcher Angela Duckworth has adopted a "hard thing rule" at home, where all members of the family have to undertake a hard thing for a minimum of six months (learning an instrument, a language, or completing a project). One of my coaching colleagues, Rich Litvin, plays the "no" game with his clients every October. Individuals have to ask other people in their lives for something outrageous, and get a thousand rejections by collecting a thousand 'no's—with no consideration for the 'yes's!

Acknowledge time on task. Australian child psychologist Dr Louise Porter is a huge proponent of acknowledgment without praise or rewards. She talks about acknowledgment as a process:

> *Verify the children's own assessment that they have achieved something worthwhile, highlight their successes so that they notice these, and expand on what they have achieved—for example, by pointing out that, not only is their block tower very high but also, when it fell down, they had another go: they can persist. This feedback allows children to "park" information about themselves in their self-concept.*

Visualise the future. Closely linked to their own goal-setting, encourage children to think weeks, months, years, and decades ahead of where they are today. Where will they be a year from now? Five years from now? What about 25 years from now? What will it take to get them there? What if it takes longer?

Press on

Calvin Coolidge, the US president from 1923 to 1929, saw persistence as the most important facet in a lifetime devoted to learning. He was also direct in expressing this:

> *Nothing in the world can take the place of persistence.*
> *Talent will not; nothing is more common than unsuccessful men with talent.*
> *Genius will not; unrewarded genius is almost a proverb.*
> *Education will not; the world is full of educated derelicts.*
> *Persistence and determination are omnipotent.*
> *The slogan "press on" has solved and always will solve the problems of the human race.*

There are now a number of gifted researchers focused on discovering more about promoting persistence and self-control. Individual efforts by parents and teachers are the front line for fostering persistence as a crucial quality in children.

While a high level of persistence won't make up for low intelligence, when high levels of persistence and intelligence are combined, the effects set a child up for life. Indeed, it is these efforts—not the actual outcomes—that count in the bigger picture. Our bright children need to be shown that their consistent efforts *are* success; that when they apply consistent, focused, deliberate, persistent effort, they have already succeeded in harnessing the power of something over which they have complete control: themselves.

Take it further

Questions for adults
- What is something you could reward yourself with when you've accomplished your next goal?
- What is your dream? Imagine you are 90 years old, looking back on your life, and you never created this dream. How does that feel to you?

Questions for children
- Think of a time when you had to try really hard to get things done. What was it like?
- What do you want to do when you grow up?
- What would it feel like when you get there?

Resources
- **Read:** Angela Duckworth and Martin Seligman's paper *Self-Discipline Outdoes IQ in Predicting Academic Performance of Adolescents.*
- **Read:** Louise Porter's article *Motivating Children.*
- **Read:** Eric Jensen and Carole Snider's book *Turnaround Tools for the Teenage Brain: Helping Underperforming Students Become Lifelong Learners.*

Q:

How should I encourage the quality of resilience in my bright child?

A:

Resilience is not a quality, it is an ongoing strategy. It can be supported by helping your bright child understand how their brain works, and by providing the necessary support.

Bright children already have the first part of resilience: innate smarts. Parents and teachers can help introduce the full formula: secure relationships, effective strategies, persistence, confidence, and a personal passion that brings the child real joy.

My long-time editor asked me a while ago about the enthusiastic and optimistic tone that echoes through all of my publications. To her, it seemed like I had never had any real problems in my life.

Of course, that couldn't be further from the truth. Every human being has to overcome hardship in life, usually in the form of devastating events or difficult personal circumstances. And of course, I have encountered a number of huge challenges as well—many of them overwhelming. Every individual on this planet will recognise at least one of my struggles: physical abuse, suicides of a brother and later a close friend, miscarriages, infidelity, near-death experiences, dismissal, financial issues, and repeated major surgery. All before the age of 30!

Here's the thing: everyone has stories like these. And I could choose to dwell on them, with predictable results if I stayed with them for too long. Indeed, some of those experiences needed a lot of space, and some needed professional assistance before bouncing back.

All of these stories highlight the power and necessity of developing a resilient and optimistic attitude—of being able to bounce back. In a 2015 survey by Australian Mensa, parents were asked about the top challenges facing their gifted children. In the survey report, "positivity and resilience" was named as a challenge for nearly a quarter of Australia's Mensan children.

And just what is resilience? The term was introduced to psychology in the 1980s by French neuropsychiatrist Boris Cyrulnik. It is the capacity to bounce back in circumstances that could otherwise lead to breakdown. (The original concept comes from physics, where it refers to a material's ability to return to its original form after being subjected to shock.) In simple language, resilience refers to the idea of springing back—just like a rubber band after stretching, a tennis ball after being hit, or a bouncy ball propelling itself back into the air.

Professor Cyrulnik explains that resilience is not a trait or quality. Instead, it is an ongoing strategy. He speaks of a "travail de résilience". This "travail" involves a child being able to distance themselves from a traumatic experience, especially through being able to view it from a "third-party" or outside perspective.

In a 2015 presentation, Norwegian psychologist Liv M. Lassen from the University of Oslo proposed a simple formula for resilience. Separately, Professor of Child Development Ann S. Masten from the University of Minnesota provides a range of factors necessary for optimal resilience. I've integrated Professor Masten's findings to develop Dr Lassen's formula further:

Resilience = Smarts + Security + Persistence + Confidence + Excitement

Here is a look at each of these factors, along with

simple practical tools that can be applied especially for bright children.

Smarts (as IQ and problem-solving skills). Bright children are at an obvious advantage with the first factor of resilience: smarts. Being able to solve problems is a key ingredient in figuring out *how* to recover from a setback. But it's only one of a variety of factors needed to bounce back. After all, we can't always "logic" our way out of many kinds of trauma, including grief or injury.

Security (in relationships)
...with parents or caregivers. In his bestselling book, *Real Love in Parenting,* Dr Greg Baer describes the absolute importance of receiving unconditional support as a child. "You can't build a solid house on a rotten, shifting foundation. But if you were not unconditionally loved as a child, that's the kind of foundation you have, and no effort you put into the walls, windows, and doors will ever be fulfilling."

I use Dr Baer's material in many of my seminars for parents of bright children. His practical concepts are applicable across different countries and cultures. They all centre around the idea of support and acceptance through *real love,* and describe the use of basic tools like listening, talking, looking (eye contact, depending on the culture), and giving time (not being "too busy").

When bright children are given this solid foundation of support and acceptance, they are more resilient when facing life's inevitable challenges.

...with others (including peers, friends, and partners). Getting parenting right is crucial. How children learn to treat others, and *how they learn to allow themselves to be treated* defines how they enter into relationships with others. This includes other adults, professionals, peers, friends, and eventually their own partners.

When bright children understand that they can rely on themselves and others—especially through experiencing this support system—they are better equipped to move through difficult times. Putting a strong focus on real friendships with real people (rather than electronics) is a great first step.

...with their environment and community. These close relationships extend to communities. As the old African saying goes, "It takes a village to raise a child". This is true when we extend parenting and outside relationships right through to schools and communities. To create effective coping and learning strategies, bright children need their own personalised ideal environment—and this is especially relevant with regards to the choice of neighbourhood and school. This environment includes the people in it, the quality and pace of living and learning, the support structure, and even the visual appeal of what's around them.

Persistence (as motivation to succeed, and to increase the level of hope and understanding). Persistence is a key part of resilience. It is defined as the quality of sticking to a task despite failures. This can be promoted in bright children through providing a real challenge, focusing on what is going right, visualising the future with them, and creating goals with ongoing feedback and discussion.

Confidence (as self-control and self-efficacy). Genuine, deep confidence can be stimulated through task stickability (persistence). Other strategies for developing confidence include helping a child discover their own strengths, giving them genuine acknowledgment instead of praise, showing them tangible evidence of success in themselves and others, and allowing a bright child to follow their own excitement and passion.

Excitement (as passion and joy). The only reason that I haven't written "excitement" as the number one factor in resilience is that the spot's already taken by the foundation of unconditional support and acceptance. However, for ongoing resilience, bright children require the recognition and realisation of their very own passion. Without an exciting passion, bright children have nothing to aim for—their bouncy ball deflates.

You may have had the experience of being in the middle of a "peak" period of life (an exciting passion) when an adverse event occurs (maybe a car fault or financial hiccup). Interestingly, in this state, we can often bounce back very quickly—perhaps not even registering the adverse event at all.

As soon as a bright child shows an interest in a particular hobby or skill, parents should provide them with support and resources to explore that to its fullest. This may mean providing them with a learning course, exposure to hands-on examples, or a mentor to guide them.

Being the ball

Author of *Flow* and popular speaker Professor Mihaly Csikszentmihalyi (pronounced *mee-high cheeks-sent-me-high*) talks about the many benefits that come from adopting a strategy of resilience.

> *Of all the virtues we can learn, no trait is more useful, more essential for survival, and more likely to improve the quality of life than the ability to transform adversity into an enjoyable challenge.*

While it's true that the world is getting better and better, bright children aren't encased in glass. Their experiences will include things failing and going wrong. The ability to bounce back requires careful support and the reinforcement of each resilience factor. Not just the child's innate smarts, but also secure relationships from parents and friends, effective strategies, persistence, confidence, and a personal passion that brings them real joy.

Take it further

Questions for adults
- How secure do you feel?
- How secure does your child feel?
- How do you deal with failure or rejection?

Questions for adults
- What's the *best thing* that has ever happened in your life—how long did that feeling last?
- What's the *worst thing* that has ever happened in your life—how long did that feeling last?
- What did you do after the *worst thing* to feel better?

Resources
- **Read:** Greg Baer's book *Real Love*.
- **Watch:** Mihaly Csikszentmihalyi's video *Flow, the secret to happiness*.
- **Watch:** Samantha Schwartz' video *Optimistic Explanatory Style*.
- **Watch:** Martin Seligman's video *Dr Martin Seligman's Adelaide lecture*.

Q:

How do I improve my child's self-esteem and confidence?

A:

A child's confidence comes from understanding themselves, feeling positive, having previous experience, and a sense of perspective.

Confidence is a requirement for bright children to communicate and thrive. Deep confidence ensures that bright children can overcome laziness, welcome discomfort, confront personal fears, be authentic, harness focus, and recognise personal values.

After a 2015 presentation I gave in Singapore to the International Coach Federation, a bubbly Singaporean woman and her American husband approached me. They wanted to know more about the kind of coaching work I did, and whether it could help their son.

"He's nine years old, and very bright. Would you be able to coach him tomorrow before you go back to Australia?" they asked. Not one to turn down any high performer, I had them schedule a time with me.

The next day, my driver pulled up to a large mansion just outside the bustling city hub. As I buzzed into the gate, a small boy bounced out from the front room of the house to greet me. "You must be Oscar!" I said, extending my hand.

Indeed it was. Oscar's confidence was evident immediately. He spoke eloquently, covering his day in school, including the new round of maths testing his class had undertaken. He drifted between a mixture of several accents—a result of his upbringing in various countries. Once his parents joined us for the session, Oscar moved easily to speaking about his latest discoveries, the concept of irrationality, and his favourite soccer players. At one point, he uncovered new solutions to one of the somatic coaching exercises, reaching a conclusion that I hadn't heard previously. We rounded out the session by talking about languages—Oscar is one of the many high performers being taught more than one language at home and at school.

Even when he didn't know the answer to something, Oscar always seemed sure of himself, secure in the knowledge that he was deserving, safe, and supported. He was a genuinely confident nine-year-old.

Confidence defined

Given the confusion—and sometimes negative perception—of self-esteem, let's start with a bunch of statements to help define a few terms: self-esteem, self-efficacy, optimism, and confidence.

I am worthy and deserving. This is one of the classic definitions of **self-esteem**, and looks at a child's relationship with themselves. We're not going to reference this one too much. I agree with Professor Martin Seligman's thesis that self-esteem is not a useful focal point on its own, cannot be taught, and that "self-esteem is a by-product of doing well".

I can achieve my own goals. Psychologists refer to this as **self-efficacy** (self-effectiveness). It looks at a child's sureness in their own abilities as both an *understanding* of their strengths, and a *trust* in themselves.

I feel positive about my life. Closely linked to these concepts, the idea of **optimism** is extremely important, as it defines a child's belief that life is generally "good", and that the world is a safe place.

Finally, **confidence** is an external expression of a

combination of these. Self-efficacy plus optimism, taking into account previous experience, and the importance of a goal or event.

Here's a way to visualise that relationship. I've developed it based on work by confidence specialist Dr Carol Craig and, later, management psychologist Dr Anna Rowley:

Confidence = "I can achieve my own goals" +
"I feel positive about my life" +
Previous experience +
Importance of goal or event

In other words, confidence appears when "I believe that I can achieve my own goals" is coupled with "I feel positive about my life", with variances based on previous experience, and how important a particular goal or event is.

The quality of confidence is highly visible; you know a confident child when you see one. They are articulate, with a dynamic and bold use of language. They have unwavering eye contact (depending on the culture). They are also comfortable with trying new things, not knowing the answer and, yes, failure. Importantly, confident children also more often know when and how to remove themselves from harmful situations (including bullying).

Confidence is a distinct quality of high performers.

High performers in the creative and arts industries have demonstrated some of the best examples of natural confidence I have ever seen. Many of them have been given an early strong foundation of support, have identified their own passions and bring optimism to their own continued success. However, in such a volatile industry (many creative performers aren't sure what their next project will be), sometimes expressing confidence deliberately is necessary. Happily, this "acting as if" has a positive strengthening effect on deeper foundations, including self-esteem.

Confidence is not a competition. Dr Nathaniel Branden (a gifted child himself) was one of the most prolific voices in the study and application of self-esteem across six decades (the 1960s through to the 2010s). He popularised the idea of the "pillars" of self-esteem, which can be visualised as supporting scaffolding for our lives. While the detail here is my own observation and experience, I have matched them against Dr Branden's original six pillars describing a person with high self-esteem:

1. **They live consciously**; their behavioural style is aligned with who they really are. They have been encouraged to understand themselves and the world they live in. They have taken the time to explore their own values and desires (what is important to them), and they live these

in their day-to-day lives.

2. **They accept themselves**; they are friends with themselves. They accept their strengths and weaknesses. They understand, from an early age, that they are not their thoughts, and that they have the power in any moment to change the world.

3. **They take responsibility for themselves**; somewhere along the way, they have been imbued with a sense of knowing their power. They realise that they get to choose which path to take, and they have the final say on their own "success" in the world (whatever that looks like to them).

4. **They are self-assertive**; they live by their own needs and desires. This includes saying "no" to things that don't align with who they really are. While understanding their worth is important, being able to walk away from circumstances that are not helpful to them is also vital.

5. **They live on purpose**; they take responsibility for themselves. This includes finding their own goals, and moving towards accomplishment.

6. **They have personal integrity**; they are loyal to themselves. This shows up in big and small ways—being on time, keeping promises, doing what they say they'll do.

In his later years, his complex and academic theories were sharpened with a more approachable edge:

> *I remember reflecting on the issue of self-esteem versus confidence one day while watching my dog play in the backyard. She was running about, sniffing flowers, chasing squirrels, leaping into the air and showing great joy (from my human perspective) in being alive. She was not thinking (I am sure) that she was more glad to be alive at that moment than the dog next door. She was simply delighting in her own existence. That moment captured something essential about my understanding of self-esteem.*

After I gave a seminar on confidence in Sydney, a woman came up to me concerned about one of her son's current challenges. As she told it, he was constantly boasting to others about his intellect and how talented he was. Her question surprised me, as she asked: "What do you do with children who have *too much* confidence?".

Though the question was justified, the concepts were misplaced. There is no such thing as too much confidence. Perhaps more important even than financial security, mental wellbeing, or physical wellness—none of which have a "ceiling"—confidence is a limitless quality.

If you notice that a child seems to have "too much confidence", consider that it may be in fact the opposite. A lack of confidence can be masked by arrogance, boasting, and "showing off".

Practical applications

After the trainwreck of the 1980s "self-esteem movement", I'd like to think that parents and teachers have learned what **not** to do.

Ways of strengthening the pillars of self-esteem indirectly include overcoming laziness, welcoming discomfort, confronting personal fears, being authentic, harnessing focus, and recognising personal values (things that we find important). We can't work directly on improving another person's self-esteem. But we can work on helping another person *do well.*

So, how can we directly help another person *do well?* By working directly on *confidence* ("I can achieve my own goals" + "I feel positive about my life" + previous experience + importance of goal or event).

Show unconditional support and acceptance (as love). Complete and unwavering support and acceptance means just that. At its face value, this means that there is no room for criticism, insults, or abuse of any kind. At a deeper level, this requires an adult who supports and accepts themselves, and is capable of supporting and accepting those around them at all times. In his book *Real Love in Parenting,* Dr Baer says: "Until a child—or an adult—is utterly convinced that he or she is loved unconditionally, even a small amount of doubt or fear is sufficient to destroy the effect of many moments of acceptance and safety."

Promote persistence. In the previous chapter on persistence, we listed many practical techniques available to parents and educators to help a child stick to a task despite failures. These techniques apply equally to promoting confidence.

By nurturing optimism at home and in the classroom (both socially and emotionally), children feel safe and supported. Through regularly listening to a child's goals and helping them to visualise the future, they are encouraged to "look ahead" and continue towards their goal. One of the first people to research this topic, Canadian–American psychologist Albert Bandura, states:

> *People's beliefs about their own abilities have a profound effect on those abilities. Ability is not a fixed property; there is a huge variability in how you perform. People who have a sense of self-efficacy [an element of confidence] bounce back from*

failures; they approach things in terms of how to handle them rather than worrying what can go wrong.

Give genuine acknowledgment. Bright children are particularly sensitive to the sincerity of this acknowledgment and can tell when it is too general or forced. Insincere praise makes a child feel invisible, may make them "addicted" to this constant positive feedback or even anxious that they may disappoint later on. Another piece of common sense was given to us by German–American psychologist Erik Erikson nearly 70 years ago:

> Children cannot be fooled by empty praise and condescending encouragement. Their identity gains real strength only from wholehearted and consistent recognition of real accomplishment.

Ensure that they are being acknowledged for a specific action (what they are doing well, and what they can build on). Finally, look for what your bright child is *doing right.* Examples include acknowledging when a child commits to a goal without giving up (encouraging persistence), and when they are telling the truth (encouraging integrity).

Show them success. Six-year-old Quentin was a bright child who loved science. He was also quiet, keeping his ideas inside his own head. With a huge capacity for learning and joining the dots, Quentin absorbed a lot of information and had some big dreams, but wasn't so good at presenting these to others.

This all changed when he was shown a YouTube video of 11-year-old American boy Peyton Robertson (mentioned earlier). Peyton had invented a new type of sandbag out of polymer, becoming "America's Top Young Scientist". In several of his online videos, Peyton is shown as a confident, articulate boy who speaks passionately about his interests. Just through watching this example of successful speaking, Quentin realised that he needed to express himself more fully to convey his ideas to the outside world.

By introducing bright children to others like them who have achieved their own goals and carry an optimistic attitude, children are better able to realise their capacity. Find resources that demonstrate *how to be*, and let children have access to these. This can include real-life mentors. More often though, it is useful to have the whole world of mentors available to draw from. Stories have been around since the dawn of time. Books improved this dissemination of information. Now, technology and devices provide a seamless way to access global inspiration.

Make way for mastery. Mastery occurs when bright children recognise themselves, and when obstacles have been removed.

Professional coaching with parental involvement is the most effective tool I've found for helping children identify and understand themselves. With a focus on individual aspects of the child (including personal strengths, talents, needs, and values) they are able to move past the "high IQ" metric (or "smart" label) and into a more tangible world of expressing their brilliance.

Putting it together. Confidence amplifies IQ, magnifies individual strengths, and deepens brilliance. In my work with hundreds of high performers over many years, the most distinctive attribute—the very first quality I notice—is confidence. It's a compelling quality precisely because it allows a child to project their *inside* world to the *outside* world. It is the surest indicator and the brightest beacon that a high performer has moved past acceleration and is actually *flying*.

Take it further

Questions for adults
- On a scale from 1 to 10, how confident do you feel right now?
- What would you be doing if you were 10 times more confident?
- How can you believe in your child in the way they most need it?

Questions for children
- What does confidence mean to you?
- Who is the most confident person you know?
- In what ways do you think being *confident* is as important as being *smart*?

Resources
- **Read (with your young child):** Byron Katie's book *Tiger-Tiger, Is It True?: Four Questions to Make You Smile Again.*
- **Read:** Carol Craig's book *Creating confidence: A handbook for professionals working with young people.*
- **Read:** Nathaniel Branden's article *Role of Adults in Bolstering a Child's Self-Esteem.*

Q:

My child is happy just playing with her friends. How can I get her to see the importance of work?

A:

Play is essential for bright children. It is one of the most effective, undeniable, clinically proven, research-based solutions for turning brightness into brilliance.

The importance of play in high-performing children cannot be understated. The ingredient of play is both pleasurable and beneficial—it is where the magic happens.

Richard loved playing. Throughout his years at school, he always came back to the simple notion of relaxing, daydreaming, and integrating play as a way of solidifying learning.

One day, while studying at Cornell University in New York, Richard was relaxing in the cafeteria.

Letting his mind wander, he noticed someone fooling around by throwing a plate in the air, and then catching it. Richard recounts this story:

> *As the plate went up in the air I saw it wobble, and I noticed the red medallion of Cornell on the plate going around. It was pretty obvious to me that the medallion went around faster than the wobbling. I had nothing to do, so I start to figure out the motion of the rotating plate... [Later] I went on to work out equations of wobbles. Then I thought about how electron orbits start to move in relativity. Then there's the Dirac Equation in electrodynamics. And then quantum electrodynamics. And before I knew it... the whole business that I got the Nobel Prize for came from that piddling around with the wobbling plate.*

The quote comes from his book, *Surely You're Joking, Mr Feynman!* And Mr Feynman—Mr Richard

Phillips Feynman—remains one of the most well-regarded physicists in the world, bringing us the theory of quantum electrodynamics, the physics of the superfluidity of supercooled liquid helium, as well as the parton model in particle physics. As an interesting side note, both that book and a later book were written from live notes recorded while Richard played bongo drums with his friend!

There are similar stories about Greek scholar Archimedes playing in his bathtub (Archimedes' principle is a law of physics fundamental to fluid mechanics), and even German physicist Albert Einstein playing on his bicycle (Einstein's theory of relativity).

Let me be super clear about this: play is absolutely crucial for creativity, innovation, new thought, and a host of other positive attributes.

Have you ever seized upon a breakthrough idea while showering, driving, or trying to drift off to sleep? I can vouch for the first two of those. The third is happening right now as I write these words: allowing my mind to rest and unwind after a long day has reminded me of several playful stories. Here's another one of my favourites...

In his celebrated book *Play,* American clinical researcher Stuart Brown writes about an issue found at Cal Tech's Jet Propulsion Laboratory (JPL). The research staff at JPL—American's major institution for aerospace research since 1936—are rocket scientists in the most literal sense.

In the late 1990s and early 2000s, JPL's managers discovered that they were having trouble recruiting good, new staff. As the older generation began retiring, it was important that the newer team could keep up.

While the interviews and CVs of the new graduates were fantastic, and JPL only hired the cream of the crop, the results of these new employees were less than stellar. The major issue JPL was seeing was a lack of *practical problem solving* from the younger team members. These new employees had the theory and maths down pat. But they couldn't take a real system with an error and break it down to find the missing piece.

The JPL management team found that the younger staff, while theoretically very capable, didn't have the childhood practical, hands-on experience necessary to excel. Perhaps they hadn't played enough with Lego, or, more likely, hadn't been allowed the time to get dirty: taking apart electronics, making mud pies, building projects from scratch.

It was only the older generation that had spent time—especially playtime—as bright children handling and shaping real-life objects like clocks, stereos, go-karts, and other appliances.

So the JPL interview process was reshaped. It now includes questions about potential employees' "free time" projects, and about their play—as children, and as adults. Professor Brown says:

> *I don't think it is too much to say that play can save your life... Life without play is a grinding, mechanical existence organised around doing the things necessary for survival. Play is the stick that stirs the drink.*

Educators are at the forefront of building free play into the school day. But even today, opportunities for physically active play in standard old schools are disappointing. In 2015 (in *Pediatrics),* a two-year study showed that American children in daycare centres and preschools only had 48 minutes of free play during the day.

In my conversations with teachers across Australia, several have noted that increasing playtime (especially through unstructured physical education time) has had positive effects in unrelated fields, including higher marks in both maths and English.

It's apparent that play is essential to a bright child. It helps them grasp problem solving in their day-to-day lives. Their effectiveness as brilliant human beings requires play for creativity in every arena.

While some of the most well-known names in history (people like Mozart, Sir Ian McKellen, and even Elon Musk) may well have spent a lot of "serious" time practising their craft, it's well documented that they were (are) also very, very playful.

We've seen what play *is* and how it is useful, but what about what play *isn't?* It's important to note that these things are NOT play:

- Overscheduling: adults often like to ensure a child doesn't get "bored" by overstimulating them. Instead, this is counter-productive.
- Screen time: especially passively absorbing entertainment (such as TV) instead of actively creating their own amusement.
- "Playing" to get a result: play is unstructured and without purpose. Adding a purpose (such as through gamification) goes against the core principles of play—a bit like trying to hide vegetables in ice-cream!

The Declaration of the Rights of the Child, adopted by the UN General Assembly Resolution 1386 (XIV) of 20 November 1959 includes a paragraph specifically about play:

> *The child shall have full opportunity for play and recreation, which should be directed to the same purposes as education; society and the public authorities shall endeavour*

to promote the enjoyment of this right.

Russian psychologist Lev Vygotsky highlights that play provides a way for children to easily recall, recreate, imagine, and experience what they have learnt. He adds that these same mental operations might be too difficult if the same children were to simply try to apply logic, reason, or discussion. Instead, they get to use their free-flowing, "relaxed" minds—with the added benefit of using their physical expression.

One of the reasons that the creative and improvisational nature of play is important is that it follows rules. Children—especially bright children—don't just do whatever they want. When a child is pretending to play house, they are abiding by all of the rules associated with what "playing house" means. Of course, because children are still learning new concepts, they will have their own different ideas about *how to play.* This brings in the essential skill of negotiation. Exploring this world of negotiation and relationships helps them process how they can change their way of being themselves in the world, and why this is useful.

Being able to effectively negotiate with each other is just one of the many well-researched outcomes of play. But playing brings life to every part of a bright child's development: **fine motor and manipulation skills** through drawing and taking things apart; **gross motor skills**, through skipping, running and kicking; **coordination**, through throwing and balancing; and **language skills** through rhyming and singing. This is on top of ongoing enhancement of cognitive capacity through problem solving, trial and error, and discarding information.

In group play, the idea of play becomes even more important. Children have the freedom to make their own decisions, including finding different paths to take during a game. This can involve complex strategies, planning, and management. Of course, **social skills** around relationships develop also. Cooperation with others, teamwork, empathy, understanding social rules, and self-control—including appropriate expression of anger or frustration—all come through group play.

Interestingly, we can promote play through lack of external stimulation, and even solitude. At first, a bright child may feel "bored". Perhaps they are accustomed to imposed structure and organisation from parents or teachers, where the mistake of creating the child's activities for them is often seen as beneficial.

However, like letting a child fail, it's useful also to let a child feel *boredom*. In this feeling of being under-stimulated, they can explore their own capacity. They can bring their true selves to the world. They can transform boredom into aliveness.

Of course, play by itself is not the answer; balance is

the key. But forgetting this important ingredient—or replacing it with structured play with the purpose of achieving—leads to potential dangers. As Professor Stuart Brown warns: "The opposite of play is not work. The opposite of play is depression."

Take it further

Questions for adults
- What would you do if you had the day off—with no stress or pressure?
- How can you increase the amount of "playtime" you give yourself?
- How do you think increased play would affect your child's education?

Questions for children
- What was the funniest thing you heard today?
- What was your favourite thing that happened today?
- What is the link between *playing* and *living?*

Resources
- **Read:** Paul Tough's article *The Make-Believe Solution.*
- **Read:** Stuart Brown's book *Play: How it Shapes the Brain, Opens the Imagination, and Invigorates the Soul.*
- **Watch:** *Richard Feynman playing bongos.*

Q:

My child has started "playing down". They can do so much more. How do I help?

A:

"Playing down" begins when children are in the wrong environment. Change the environment.

Another key ingredient for high performance is "playing full out", not "playing down". It's easy to notice when a child has decided to play down, or opt out of life. It's also the perfect time to help them find a resolution.

Triceratops. Stegosaurus. Tyrannosaurus Rex. Diplodocus. Iguanodon.

Even though she was just three years old, Isabelle could pronounce the full names of all the greatest dinosaurs, and knew the differences between them. She knew why an Ichthyosaurus was classed as a reptile, and not a dinosaur. She could also describe the structure of a Gastonia (both her mum and I had to look that one up—it was definitely a dinosaur!).

The school system in England starts slightly earlier than most of the rest of the world. In fact, children can begin "nursery" during the first school term after their third birthday.

So Isabelle began, in England, her introduction to schooling—and to one of the challenges of being bright—at the tender age of three. Surrounded by other children her own age, Isabelle began conversations about dinosaurs with anyone she could. Or at least, she tried to. Her efforts were rewarded with grunting from the other toddlers.

Can you imagine what it feels like to be in a situation where you are completely surrounded by other humans who won't or can't communicate with you?

I wrote about this feeling in my first book, *Best*. Here's an excerpt:

> *Orangutans are the smartest creature besides humans, and have been tested*

using the same IQ scale as for humans, reportedly achieving results between 49–90. Of course, the scale is designed for humans not animals, and certainly doesn't take into consideration things like culture and creativity.

Humans can fit anywhere on the scale, but usually sit somewhere between 50 and 150. The baseline, 100, is adjusted frequently to take into account the new population...

The middle of the bell curve then, is the "average" human. The 100. The Joe Bloggs.

... [On the right-hand side] of the bell curve, above 130, is where genius lies. Genius...

If we take nothing else besides IQ into account then, what is particularly interesting to note is that the difference between a genius and Joe Bloggs is the same as the difference between Joe Bloggs and an orangutan...

And it's fun living with orangutans! It's fun playing with them, trying to communicate with them, seeing them eat and watching them live their lives.

But there does come a time when it gets tiring playing with the orangutans all day. There is a real world out there waiting. Orangutans don't have hovercrafts or deep conversation or investment opportunities or cinema or any of the other things that make us... us.

Isabelle's IQ score sits somewhere between 165 and 171, depending on the type of test. And yet her nursery placed her in the same "bucket" as 30 other toddlers who hadn't yet learnt to pronounce the word "dinosaur". (Former American president Thomas Jefferson noted: "There is nothing so unequal as the equal treatment of unequal individuals.")

So in the middle of this sea of grunting inequality, and still as a three-year-old, Isabelle had just a few options.

Option number one was to **remove herself from the environment**. Not an easy task as a child. Isabelle tried to escape from the nursery several times.

Option number two was to get the attention of those around her by **misbehaving or "acting out":** she could let the world know that she was not flourishing. This choice to misbehave is one of the only outlets that children can see. Of course, this resulted in her spending a lot of time in the naughty chair. With no direct training in working with gifted children, her teachers remained unsympathetic.

So, Isabelle reverted to a fascinating third option; a way of being that many adults revert to as well. She began **playing down**.

Isabelle went from conversations about animals, birds, and fossils, to something much different. Her mum reports that Isabelle began using baby talk.

Discussions which had previously been about the Jurassic period were replaced with baby language like "mama". And where once Isabelle had fluent answers to thorny adult questions, her new response was, "I don't know."

Her parents were devastated. Within weeks, they had taken advice from a child psychologist, and moved Isabelle into home-schooling. Her behaviour changed back nearly overnight.

Do you know of someone who plays down? Who tries to "blend in" so that they won't cause a fuss?

The idea of playing down cannot possibly serve a bright child, nor indeed anyone.

The concept of playing down—deliberately handicapping one's own passion, confidence, walk, presence, choice of friends, talking, and happiness—is *terrifying*.

Indeed, there is an emotional cost to playing down what we know to be our authentic self. Making the choice to become invisible, or to camouflage our real selves, certainly helps to avoid the issue of social isolation.

But it uncovers an even greater issue. Camouflaging and pretending withholds our greatest self from those around us. Much worse, it can eventually become self-alienation—literally becoming a stranger to our self.

Picture a cheetah slowing down so that the other animals can keep up.

Imagine a peacock choosing to tone down its colours to make the other birds feel more comfortable.

Or a giraffe crouching a little so that he doesn't stick out so much.

Our children are coming from a place of immensity, an endless well of uniqueness. It takes special guidance to ensure that they continue to bring their power and completeness to every situation; to *allow* them to be themselves so that they *can* be themselves.

There's a happy continuation for Isabelle. By the age of seven, she has found a public school with specialist gifted teachers (the principal has a gifted family of her own). Here, she is treated as "special needs"—because she is! She is given personalised lessons in Latin, high-school chemistry, and specialist subjects (including pharmaceuticals and immunisation in Third World countries). Her current goal is to win a Nobel Prize, making advances in the same fields as Einstein.

Take it further

Questions for adults
- What part of your child's situation is under your control, and what isn't?
- What can you do about the part you can change?
- What about the part you can't change?

Questions for children
- What is the link between being smart and having friends?
- How do you like to learn?
- What do you want to learn about next?

Resources
- **Watch:** *Alice Fredenham singing 'My Funny Valentine'.*
- **Watch:** *2013 Young Scientist Challenge Winner: Peyton Robertson.*

Q:

What does "moving out of the way" of bright children actually mean?

A:

Moving out of the way means removing roadblacks, *making way* for brilliance without *getting in the way*. This is paramount to a child's success.

Bright children figure it out on their own—that's what they're specially wired to do. Having the room to do what they need to is the next ingredient in high performance. When well-meaning others get in the way, it can block their free-flowing potential. It can also be dangerous…

There is a fantastic Monty Python sketch (from their *Flying Circus* series) that I used to watch over and over when I was young. The sketch is called "Gumby Brain Specialist", and features a brain-damaged brain surgeon (John Cleese) trying to operate on a patient. It includes the brain surgeon looking in the patient's pants for his brain, and a lot of general incompetence. I ended up working with John years later (another high performer), but I was reminded of this sketch recently while reading about a real-life event...

One of my favourite authors, Tim Ferriss, tells a story of being rushed to hospital in India. He and his girlfriend had eaten some bad fish at a local restaurant. Soon, they came down with fever, diarrhoea, and vomiting. They took themselves to an emergency room (and then a clinic) in Calcutta.

Here, the staff—from nurses through to surgeons—proved themselves incompetent. From taking Tim's underarm temperature through his shirt, to refusing to provide toilet paper, to switching patient charts, to inserting the IV incorrectly (injecting litres of fluid into tissue instead of a vein), Tim was surrounded by gross—and dangerous—ineptitude.

So, as Tim tells it, he started taking matters into his own hands. This was especially difficult, because he was reliant on the medical staff for everything: "To maintain hawk-like spider-sense while incapacitated, quality-controlling everything to avert disaster, is taxing beyond belief." Even in his delirium, he started instructing the doctors on what to do, and how to do it. When the IV wasn't flowing into his arm properly, Tim says: "I used sign language to show they'd forgotten to put an additional needle in the IV bottle to create necessary vacuum and flow."

In one situation, his girlfriend collapsed from a violent reaction to a drug administered by the doctors. Tim repeatedly told the doctors not to give her any more of the drug. Later that night, Tim told the head doctor, who promised to relay the message to the other staff in the clinic. A few hours later, Tim had to restrain a nurse who was again about to inject his girlfriend with the drug.

In the end, Tim's awareness saved both of their lives, and they recovered. The whole scenario—placing a bright leader in a sea of incompetence—is a fantastic metaphor for the situation that many of our bright children can find themselves in.

Well-meaning professionals. Outgoing peers learning and teaching new things. Even family. While all of these are beautiful in their own right, bright children *think differently.*

Is it any wonder that many of them choose to isolate themselves from outside forces that tend to bring them down, and even expose them to danger? In his article *Prodigies' Oddities*, Chris Wayan makes a similar comparison: "Picture yourself stuck in a bed on life support run by a team of brain-damaged doctors... and maybe you can see where the prodigy's go-it-alone syndrome comes from!".

The reasoning behind the all-too-familiar response of self-imposed isolation, or at least "taking care of oneself" is incontrovertible. Bright children may not always know *best*—they are, after all, still children—but they nearly always know *better!*

I often speak about "moving out of the way" of bright children. Sometimes parents are confused by this. We should support, accept, and love... and then get out of the way? The idea may seem a little harsh at first. But there is a more gentle meaning behind it: allow your child to be their best selves. Remove obstacles, stand back, and let bright children flourish—including letting them fail.

Because, for all your love and care in steering a bright child to get where they need to go, it is not up to others to try and steer them. A bonfire doesn't need to be forced to practise the violin. A lightning bolt doesn't need to sit in a jail cell to be taught the periodic table. And a bright child doesn't need to be shown how to live in a cage.

In his book *Antifragile,* Nassim Nicholas Taleb quotes Edward Osborne Wilson in describing the biggest hindrance to a child's development. Veering into provocation, he names "the soccer mom".

> *They repress children's natural biophilia, their love of living things. But the problem is more general; soccer moms try to eliminate the trial and error, the antifragility, from children's lives, move them away from the ecological and transform them into nerds working on preexisting (soccer-mom-compatible) maps of reality. Good students, but nerds—that is, they are like computers except slower. Further, they are now totally untrained to handle ambiguity. As a child of civil war, I disbelieve in structured learning... Provided we have the right type of rigor, we need randomness, mess, adventures, uncertainty, self-discovery, near-traumatic episodes...*

More generally, any forced and artificial attempts to drive a child are just that—forced. These attempts at guiding are futile at best, and dangerous at worst.

They succeed in only one thing: *getting in the way.*

With the support of being seen, listened to, and accepted completely, brightness finds its own path. Drop the utensils and the polishing cloths. Leave an open environment for it to be revealed.

Move out of the way.

Take it further

Questions for adults
- In what ways do you *get in the way* of your bright child?
- How could this be holding back both yourself and your child?
- What do you believe about your child's future, based on what you've seen so far? (Express it!).

Questions for children
- If you were bigger and louder and couldn't fail, how would the world look different?
- When you are your best, you are _____ (fill in the blank).
- Imagine that you are 100 years old, telling a story to your own grandchildren about your achievements in life. What would you tell them?

Resources
- **Read:** Nassim Nicholas Taleb's book *Antifragile: Things That Gain from Disorder.*

Q:

How do I choose the best school for my bright child?

A:

Become deeply involved in finding a personalised learning environment for your child.

Most schools are not designed for bright children. School is for socialising and learning valuable life skills. Many bright children acquire most of their knowledge on their own: they are self-driven. It is vital that education is tailored to their strengths.

I had a friend who used to work at McDonald's. She started at the age of 14. Every day, she would go to work, clock in, and serve customers.

She performed routine tasks. She was provided with standard training on "how to flip burgers" and "how to smile at customers". She was paid the standard hourly rate.

This girl was definitely bright. She didn't belong in a McDonald's. She knew that. I knew that. It wasn't the right fit for her. My friend used her time to learn some relevant business skills, and then moved on to other career choices—including starting her own business.

Here are some things she didn't do while working for the fast food chain:

- She didn't rant about the lack of opportunities provided by the corporation.
- She didn't post to social media about how "unfair" her company was.
- She didn't campaign for employees to be given extension programs.
- She didn't scream at her boss for not paying her enough.
- She didn't hold meetings with senior managers about the inadequacy of the work environment, and how it wasn't catering to her needs.
- She didn't bang her head against a brick wall.

As far as I'm aware, her parents didn't do any of those things either.

In fact, it is absurd to expect a corporation like McDonald's to meet any of those expectations. They are a fast-food store. They cater to a particular demographic, filling a particular need, to benefit shareholders. Employment at McDonald's is helpful for learning some business, customer service, and social skills.

I see some parents doing some (or all) of these things to their children's schools.

Here's the kicker: many standard schools have *a lot* in common with McDonald's. They are designed for the "average" pupil. They cater to the "average" pupil, filling a particular need, to benefit "average" students (not bright students). Education at a standard school is helpful for learning some life, relationship, and social skills.

It is an enormous waste of time to try to shift a corporation to provide *tailored employment*. It is an equal waste of time to try to shift a standard school to provide *tailored learning*. That's time that could be better spent looking at other options.

It's not just the choice between school types. In Australia, there seems to be constant debate over public versus private schooling. This is a terribly flawed argument.

Unfortunately, no type of standard mainstream education will ever be enough for a bright child. The current standard education system is just that: standard.

Consider the train systems in New South Wales, Australia, today. There is some truth to the oft-repeated legend that our modern railway track gauge, the distance between parallel tracks, is based on the width of two horses. The New South Wales implementation of "standard gauge" tracks is 1.435 metres.

It was adopted there in 1846, and hasn't (won't be) changed. Working backwards, we copied the English standard, adopted in 1830. The English kept a standard that went much further back. Researchers have uncovered the same 1.435-metre gauge right back to the times when wagons were used by the Roman Empire. "Standard gauge" works great for trains! For the most part, it is one international standard based on something that worked a long time ago. Trains can be designed, imported, and operated because of this standard. They can easily travel from point A to point B.

But what if your child isn't a train? And a bright child is not, by any definition, a train. They are closer to a supercar, a jet, or a space shuttle. I've worked with some brilliant children here in Australia who somehow seem to have travelled through time to be here!

Trains don't get exposure to fundamentals like financial literacy, imagination, negotiation, emotional intelligence and communication, stress management, critical thinking, or resilience. More importantly, bright children want to learn about specific fields that interest them. They want to learn about things that they are obsessed with and that they will use to change the world. Beginning, of course, with their own world.

The good news is that there are many other options to complement standard education, to accelerate flourishing. In fact, there is an entire universe available now. More reliable resources are available for bright children now than at any other time in the history of the world. And I'm not talking about Minecraft...

School options like Montessori and Steiner allow students to follow their curiosity by exploring and playing. The people that emerge from these environments are proud testaments to the basic human rights of freedom, dignity, and play.

Indeed, the Declaration of the Rights of the Child, which I mentioned earlier, puts these in writing. It states that every child:

> *Shall be given opportunities and facilities, by law and by other means, to enable him to develop physically, mentally, morally, spiritually and socially in a healthy and normal manner and in conditions of freedom and dignity.*

Shall be given an education which will promote his general culture and enable him, on a basis of equal opportunity, to develop his abilities, his individual judgement, and his sense of moral and social responsibility, and to become a useful member of society.

More than a century ago, Albert Einstein spent a year at a Pestalozzi-inspired school, later crediting the school with giving him the freedom to begin his first thought experiments on the theory of relativity. More recently, Google founders Larry Page and Sergey Brin recognised their Montessori school for imbuing them with a spirit of creativity and independence.

I work with bright children and families from all types of educational systems: public, private, specialist, and home-school. The type is not especially important. Let's take a closer look at how traditional learning environments can become a challenge—and even a barrier—to a bright child being able to learn effectively.

The challenge

Imagine waking up tomorrow as a six-year-old. You have all of your current adult intelligence, adult knowledge, and ways of processing. You even get to keep your usual power of speech. The only difference is that your birth certificate now lists you as being born six years ago—and you physically present to the world as a six-year-old.

At school, you are placed into classes with others of your age group (a colleague calls this "chronological apartheid"). Teachers talk down to you. You are essentially forced to relearn the alphabet, how to count numbers, and many other topics you've already mastered...

Sound like a nightmare? What would you do? Who would you go to?

At best, inappropriately designed education is irrelevant in the lives of high-performing children. At worst, it is a form of taking a person's life away. Nearly 100 years ago, American gifted psychologist Leta Hollingworth told us: "In the ordinary elementary school situation, children of 140 IQ waste half their time in school. Those above 170 IQ waste almost all their time."

The truth is that there is no such thing as the "perfect" school for a high performer. While several of the schools I work with are incredibly progressive, nothing can take the place of personalised, tailored learning. High performers require individualised resources to cater to their advanced and "1 in 7 billion" brains. Even the notable Mensa Gymnázium, Mensa's own—and only—grammar school (based in the Czech Republic) cannot completely meet the unique and individual needs of high performers. That's not what school is for!

Instead, it's about providing personalised learning—and then moving out of the way. In an interview with ABC Australia about providing tailored education to students, I put it in even simpler terms: "What learning style (or modality) does that child have? What growth environment do they need, and what are their specific talents? We're not teaching astronomers how to play a concerto, or musicians all about pure mathematics, it's actually about what they need to learn and what they want to learn."

Facing the right direction

If you've ever had to deal with institutions with fixed mindsets, the following true story from my first book, *Best,* may resonate. Situated in the middle of Paradise Valley, Arizona, architectural genius Frank Lloyd Wright's own winter home is a monument to dealing with (or avoiding) bureaucracy. Established in 1937, Frank designed the building to capture the sweeping views of the valley below.

A few years into the construction, the state government installed huge power lines on giant steel towers directly in front of his home, obstructing his view of paradise. Frank was indignant. He communicated his exasperation (and requests for alternatives) to anyone that would listen: the local council all the way up to then-President Truman.

Unsurprisingly, the slow and heavy institutions could do very little to help Frank. They wouldn't consider burying or relocating the power lines. In fact, they couldn't consider his requests at all—it just wasn't part of their way of thinking.

So Frank began the process for what he considered to be the only thing left available to him: he started packing up to rebuild everything again in another location. However, his partner convinced him to reconsider. There was another option: Frank and his team could take their focus away from the giant towers. They could adjust their attention instead to the beautiful mountain ranges behind them.

They had been looking the wrong way the whole time! The team did change their focus, turning their back on the valley to look instead at the beautiful McDowell Mountain Range behind the home. Of course, this meant altering their own previously fixed mindsets (and windows!).

The self-driving child

Gifted parents being frustrated by schools is not a particularly new occurrence; bright children and high performers have been under-served for some time now. It's just that the resolution is more urgent and apparent than ever before. As our world moves rapidly through the Creative Revolution, high performers without adequate and unconditional support risk being left behind, wasting time, or giving up completely.

Here's the thing: high performers are generally self-driving. They don't *require* a standard old school (SOS) to help them learn.

High performers learn autonomously and independently unless they're deliberately or inadvertently held back.

While high performers can be many years ahead of their chronological age, young children still rely on parents to steer them in the right direction. Your inspired involvement in your child's life is your responsibility. (And don't worry. I say a similar thing to teachers. To professionals. To governments. We are all responsible!).

If your child isn't performing in school, it is your responsibility to do everything in your power to resolve that. If the educational environment isn't flexible enough to change for your child, then move quickly to find a new educational environment. American educational consultant Otto Siegel says: "If the fish is sick, you need to exchange the water."

There is an array of options available to high performers in schools. The benefits of acceleration—moving students through the traditional curriculum more quickly—have been accepted conclusively by researchers and governments for many years. The 2004 American report *A Nation Deceived* identified 18 types of acceleration, nearly all of which are available to Australian children (depending on state guidelines). If your school doesn't offer these, get out! If they do, take full advantage of anything you can to provide support to your high performer.

Inspired involvement

If you're making a decision about which school to send your child to, get deeply involved. Meet the teachers. Interview the principal and staff at the school. Do they love their life, or are they stuck in a mindset from the Industrial Revolution?

Whether or not the environment is nurturing and inspiring to your child will *always* be apparent to those looking for it. Take it all in. Give less importance to the school's brand or statistics. Listen for the things that really matter, especially those things that give you a strong feeling. Teachers' voices. The tone of emails and letters. The experiences of other high performers in the environment. And *especially* feedback from your child. Look and feel every little thing.

Even the physical state of the school itself is an indicator. American coach Bill Cumming says: "When I visit schools around the country, I can tell by the condition of a building, if the possibility of being inspired is discussed in these halls. Regardless of the age of a building, they can be kept in spectacular condition. Wax shines old floors as well as new and windows never tire of being cleaned..."

Once you have found a school environment that inspires and challenges your child—or if you are one of the significant number of parents who choose to teach their high-performing child through home-schooling—then you have already discovered part of the resolution to the challenge.

The focus

Right now, and more publicly visible than at any other time in human history, high performers are called to unleash their creative potential and find their place in life. In this decade, and through the 2020s, 2030s, and 2040s, creative high performers will lead the charge.

We've got enough testing. We've got enough forced education. We've certainly had enough SOS calls from high performers who are stuck. Like Frank, we've been facing the wrong way, looking in the wrong direction. Increasing and improving out-dated educational models should not, and must not, be the focus.

The focus is on seeing brilliance in every person, accepting and supporting the massive capability inherent in each child.

The focus is on providing inspired environments for all children—especially high performers.

The focus is on listening to the needs of the limitless unique personalities in front of us.

The focus is on moving out of the way, removing obstacles, and allowing high performers the freedom to choose resources based on their interests, talents, and strengths.

Take it further

Questions for adults
- What is the best possible outcome for your child?
- If you saw yourself as powerful instead of powerless, what would you change about your child's education?
- What else could you do?

Questions for children
- What is the best part about school?
- What is the worst part about school?
- What is the difference between *school* and *learning*?

Resources
- **Read:** the Gifted Education, Research Resource and Information Centre's paper *Releasing the Brakes for High-Ability Learners: Administrator, Teacher and Parent Attitudes and Beliefs That Block or Assist the Implementation of School Policies on Academic Acceleration.*
- **Read:** Bill Cumming's article *Inspired Environments, Part 2.*

Q:

How do I know if my child's teacher is the right one for my bright child?

A:

The right teacher for your child will be able to support your child's passions, and develop an emotional connection with your child. This will enable bright children to learn to love learning.

The right teacher is another vital ingredient for high performance.

Clara is a 10-year-old girl from Kansas City, Missouri. She is part of the 10 percent of US students that attend private schools—in this case, a Montessori school. Her teacher, Kenneth Boehr, places a premium on "hands-on" learning.

One science lesson, her teacher passed out "ball-and-stick" modelling kits to build molecules. As the name suggests, these consist of brightly coloured balls and sticks, which can be plugged together to symbolise the makeup of different molecules, like water or ethanol.

Clara set to work, playing with the shapes, and randomly arranging a number of black, red, and blue balls (carbon, oxygen, and nitrogen respectively). When she had completed her model, she asked her teacher if it was a real molecule.

It was! After some research and help from a university, her creation was identified as a unique and viable chemical. Both Clara and her teacher were credited with discovering the new molecule, called "Tetranitratoxycarbon". Both teacher and student were also included in a research paper published about the chemical.

While there is a lot to take away from this story, the highlight for me is the teacher. Consider the situation where Clara is instead ignored. Or worse, belittled.

Instead, this teacher chose to bring the best out of both himself and the student. To me, this is the idea of *excellence* in teaching. It is based on four things:

1. The student's passion.
2. The teacher's passion.
3. The student's self-image.
4. The teacher's image of the student.

The student's passion

Generally, bright children want to learn. They are eager to devour information. They bring a sense of wonder with them into every moment, especially in their field of obsession. Hildegard Debringum's famous quote is hardly applicable to children: "We must each learn to hang out in the green, growing edges of our own becoming." They are always hanging out in their bliss. Do they bring this passion with them into the learning environment? Is someone inspiring them there?

The teacher's passion

This is one of the things I push to my bright families: instead of looking for a **school**, look for a **teacher**. Find one that resonates with you. It's not so much about the history, or the labels of public/private, it is always about the people. Are they inspiring? Do they want to impart knowledge? John F Podojil's famous book *I am A Teacher* includes his quote: "Teaching is not a profession; it's a passion... passion for your subject and a desire for your students to learn and be the best in the world..."

The student's self-image

There is no other human facet that more affects the outcome of a child's life than their self-image. It's the way they see themselves, their confidence in their own abilities. A little differently, it's their perceived *sense of deserving*. One of the people involved with developing the early concept of coaching, Jack Welch, says: "Giving people self-confidence is by far the most important thing that I can do. Because then they will act." And there is no greater gift you could give yourself and those around you than this confidence, and a healthy self-image. Of course, this is influenced by the people around the student. Which brings us to the last of these...

The teacher's image of the student

The role of an effective teacher is not to force-feed into brains (although rote learning does have its place). Teachers who see their students as fully capable and powerful are true teachers. Their enthusiasm ignites the fire of purpose, allowing complete aliveness.

In their default state—from birth—bright children love learning. Fuelling this love of learning to become a lifelong pursuit begins with seeing them and listening to them. Support them in recognising an individual passion, and select a learning environment where they are not intimidated or bored by their teacher. Provide an environment where they are accepted, supported, and *challenged.*

See. Listen. Provide resources for the child who is asking for them.

Take it further

Questions for adults
- What kind of emotional connection does your child have with their teacher?
- How might this affect their learning?
- What steps can you take to improve this?

Questions for children
- Who is your favourite teacher? What is it about them that makes them your favourite?
- Who is the most important person to help you learn? What makes them the most important?

Resources
- **Read:** Barbara Sand's article *Teaching genius: The teaching principles of Dorothy Delay.*
- **Read:** Steve Chandler's book *Fearless: Creating the Courage to Change the Things You Can.*
- **Watch:** the movie *Good Will Hunting.*

Q:

My bright child loves music. What's the link?

A:

For the advanced brain, music is linked to greater memory retention, deeper concentration, and higher performance.

Listening to music is another valuable ingredient of high performance. Music can inspire, enliven, and provide emotional resonance.

Having spent more than a decade working with high performers as a sound designer has allowed me to deeply appreciate the indescribable magic of music. I also continue to provide music during all coaching sessions as well, even just as barely perceptible background piano pieces. In the gifted education space, progressive educational consultants like Ian Byrd use music in the classroom as both background music and transitions: short musical clips are played before a change in subject, giving the bright students a cue to change gears.

Music has always been an essential part of being. And there are two ways of *being* in the world: creating (producing something new), and consuming (experiencing things that have already been brought to life). Although creating music has a significant relationship with brightness in children—a 2015 survey of children in Australian Mensa found that more than half of them play a musical instrument—it is not the focus of this chapter.

Consuming and listening to music, for pleasure or to help with increased processing, also benefits bright children. For all the research into music listening as it relates to neuroscience and the brain, it is not yet widely understood. There is certainly a lot of research on the benefits of listening to music as pain relief: hundreds of studies in the mainstream medical literature. Still, there is very little scientific consensus about how the brain processes music, and even less about how it affects peak performance—especially in those with advanced brains.

Neuroscientists like Professor Daniel Levitin give us quotes that get us a little closer: "Music communicates to us emotionally through systematic violations of expectations." But this doesn't really articulate the sheer power of music in our lives. The closest possible description I've found is from musician Bruce Springsteen: "Music is magic. It's the real thing. Music is not a trick. It's actual alchemy... one and one makes three. Nobody knows what that third element is going to be, but it's the one thing that matters most."

Exciting the brain, enhancing attentiveness, boosting performance

Consider the famous physicist John Von Neumann, estimated to have a very high IQ (160+). Though he is best known for his contributions to maths and physics, John had a deep appreciation for music. It was a key ingredient in allowing his brain to process and analyse information. He relied on music to turn off the world around him.

His obituary in *LIFE* magazine states that he preferred thinking while on a nightclub floor, at a lively party, or with a phonograph playing in the room, all ways to help his subconscious solve difficult problems.

> *Von Neumann believed that concentration alone was insufficient for solving some of the most difficult mathematical problems and that these are solved in the subconscious. He would often go to sleep with a problem unsolved, wake up in the morning and scribble the answer on a pad he kept by the bedside table. It was a common occurrence for him to begin scribbling with a pencil and paper in the midst of a nightclub floor show or a lively party, "the noisier," his wife says, "the better... he did most of his work in the living room with my phonograph blaring."*

While tenured at Princeton, John would often play loud German marching tunes on his office gramophone player. He did this while he himself was processing information, and while his colleagues (including Professor Albert Einstein) were also trying to work.

The most recent research related to music and peak performance points out the boost available across a broad range of measurable points. In 2013, Dr Emma Gray looked at the effect that listening to music had on students. She found that those who listened to classical music while studying performed 12 percent better during exam time. Specifically, the melody and tone range in classical music "helps students to study for longer and retain more information."

This was echoed in 2015 by research led by sports psychologist Richard Collins. The team ran a study addressing peak performance in swimmers, finding that: "tracks with an emotional resonance can boost performance and endurance as much as 10 percent." Australian Professor Peter Terry adds that music can help people to work harder for longer by masking the objective level of effort.

Loudness and content

Just what is it that makes music magic? For simplicity, there are two concepts that are useful here: loudness and content.

Loudness is exciting because it is linked to survival. Loudness reminds us of the power necessary to create a big noise, like chopping down a tree or causing a landslide. American researcher Barry Blesser, an expert on aural architecture, says: "it is clear that loud music changes the mood and behaviour of listeners, often in a pleasurable way. There may not be consistency among individuals with different temperaments and values, but the seductive attraction of loud music has a simple explanation: it does something pleasurable for listeners even if the details are not known or vary among individuals."

How we respond to content (rather than loudness) also depends on the listener. Although there are universal qualities preferred within musical content, the appreciation of music remains a subjective experience. For productivity, my high-performing clients list favourite genres from African tribal drumming through to Baroque music.

Appreciation of musical content isn't limited to only the technical makeup of music: tone, timbre, and texture. Like Springsteen's assertion that "one and one makes three", there's something underneath, an unknown element of conveyed emotion. How much of the creator's (or composer's) emotions are inside the music? And how much of this is communicated directly to the listener? A number of studies have been conducted in this area. The bottom line is that positive, uplifting music will resonate with the listener and can produce the same feeling in whatever the listener is creating.

And negative or agitating music? Professor Levitin has an interesting aside: "Wagner has always disturbed me profoundly, and not just his music, but also the *idea* of listening to it. I feel reluctant to give into the seduction of music created by so disturbed a mind and so dangerous (or impenetrably hard) a heart as his, for fear that I may develop some of the same ugly thoughts."

Of course, music is a very personal experience across the board. Several of my clients report needing the stimulation of listening to the same track on repeat, bringing them into a trance-like, meditative state. Overstimulation is possible as well (the American Academy of Paediatrics warns that loud music can overstimulate children with attention deficit hyperactivity disorder), and should certainly be taken into account.

For those bright children that are ready for it, music is a key ingredient for high performance. When they are allowed to select their own pieces to listen to, when they are encouraged to apply this powerful ingredient, they can increase their enjoyment of performance at the same time.

Take it further

Questions for adults
- How has music affected your life?
- Think about a few of your favourite songs. Do they bring back happy memories? How do you think the memories and music are linked?

Questions for children
- What is your favourite song, and why?
- What is the most interesting musical instrument?

Resources
- **Read:** Daniel Levitin's book *This Is Your Brain on Music: The Science of a Human Obsession.*
- **Read:** Barry Blesser's article *The Seductive (Yet Destructive) Appeal of Loud Music.*
- **Watch:** PBS' video *The Music Instinct.*

Q:

My bright child isn't using his full capacity, and keeps sabotaging himself. What's going on?

A:

When a child has their personal brilliance revealed, they come alive, and self-sabotage disappears.

When a bright child understands that they have the power to create their own lives, they have discovered another ingredient for high performance.

With a broad range of clients across different disciplines, interests, and cultures, most of them have one thing in common: high ability being translated into high performance.

During the *Blueprint* coaching program—or even sometimes as a standalone program—I often ask older child clients to complete an activity called "Lifewrite". This process was originally designed by Australian coach and author Michael Domeyko Rowland. In his bestselling book *Absolute Happiness*, Michael outlines how this works. It involves writing down where you want to go, what you want to do, and who you want to be over the next few years. It covers every aspect of life, from family to material possessions to emotional and spiritual wellbeing. He calls the process of writing these things down: "the single most important technique you will ever do", adding, "it is far easier to create the experiences you want when you are able to describe them with clarity."

Older children do a spectacular job of scripting their Lifewrites: several pages of detailed goals and narrative, describing new and enjoyable life experiences over the next several years. It is thrilling to hear what they have decided to create, especially specifics like choice of breakfast food, type of vehicle, or material possessions that are personal to them.

While debriefing the document with them during the process, it's often important to reinforce that our *thoughts* become our *words* become our *reality*, and that this written process is very real, and will bring these things into their experience. Not as some woo-woo new-age quackery, but as a widely accepted and proven method (now also being pushed by popular clinical psychologist Professor Jordan Peterson in his "Future Authoring Program").

While the idea of adding balance—or even negativity—might seem like a quirky thing to write into a Lifewrite, the very act of putting it down on paper embeds it firmly in the mind as something that will be brought about. That's why it is so important to only write about the experiences that they wish to create. They alone hold the responsibility for what they choose to create, and how their lives unfold. Not their parents. Not their teachers. Not society.

I ask the child to pay particular attention over the following few months or years as their lives unfold from the written story that they have created. There is an obvious connection between this *writing exercise* and their *real life*. They imagine, write, rehearse, and then act out their own experiences—positive or negative. I'm not surprised when clients tell me—years later—that both big and small things came to pass from descriptive stories they wrote in their Lifewrite. Powerful stuff!

American child psychologist Dr Maureen Neihart, in her book *Peak Performance for Smart Kids,* tells us:

> *The popular saying, "Think positive," is supported by the research on imagery and mental rehearsal. Essentially anything your children would like to do better will be helped by mental rehearsal... It's like a mini roadmap. It provides a picture of where one wants to go and how to get there.*

Bright children have the power to change their own lives. Bright children can self-sabotage (or "self-handicap") as a way of protecting themselves from the pain of taking on responsibility for their failures.

But with such strong foundations from their advanced brains they should be encouraged to create the best possible lives for themselves.

There are smatterings of conversation around this topic, but very few of them cover the specific needs of bright children. This is not about effort. Neither is this just about having a growth mindset.

Often, it is a lack of understanding of their absolute power over their lives. The difference between brightness and brilliance is often this realisation: *I am powerful enough to create something valuable to me.* When this responsibility is understood and brought to life, everything changes. A high performer is created.

Creating their best possible life is about a child being able to realise their own innate capacity—and their personal responsibility for being able to create something powerful.

Parents, educators, and professionals can integrate this vital understanding into their support of bright children, to ensure that they recognise that they have fundamental responsibility for how their lives turn out and for what they create in their own experience. For all the research that has been conducted on giftedness and performance over the last 100 years, this core understanding sticks out.

As parents, it can be useful to watch for any smouldering indications of self-sabotage, and extinguish them immediately. If you notice distracting behaviours, excuses, or negativity, help your child to turn it around. It's fascinating how quickly negativity can be turned into positive, empowering thoughts by "drawing out" their current thoughts and feelings.

Parents can also help bright children to aim for excellence rather than perfection or "pleasing others". Self-sabotage is common when bright children are trying to do well just to prevent disapproval from parents, teachers, and others around them. When they move toward excellence instead of pleasing, they are more motivated to learn, flourish, and mature.

In a presentation to the 2015 International Conference on Illuminating the Spectrum of Giftedness and Talent Development held in Brisbane, Australia, Professor Miraca Gross told the attendees:

The most effective gifted children consider themselves responsible for their own development, and they understand that they alone are the prime factor in their own academic success or failure.

When bright children see and understand the link between their *thinking* and their *performance*, they open up a whole new world of effectiveness. This means that they are responsible for all parts of their own growth, including these five aspects:

1. Passion: their own joyful and inspired commitment to where they are going.
2. Education: their own willingness to learn new things.
3. Goal-setting: their own focused attention and persistence to achieve what they want.
4. Connection: their own power to bring themselves into relationships with others.
5. Resilience: their own methods for coping with trauma, stress, and anxiety, and being optimistic.

Although it is easy for a child to blame others—parents, educators, professionals—for their effectiveness, the earlier that a bright child or young adult realises their own role in affecting their own lives, the earlier they can perform at their highest level and begin creating something important to themselves.

Take it further

Questions for adults
- What have you already accomplished that should be celebrated? (List them.)
- What will you be creating in your life five years from now?
- How could your own accomplishments inspire your bright child?

Questions for children
- What decisions do you make every day?
- What other decisions would you like to make?
- What would the world look like if everyone were creating something beautiful?

Resources
- **Read:** Carol Dweck's article *Carol Dweck Revisits the Growth Mindset.*
- **Read:** Michael Domeyko Rowland's book *Absolute Happiness: The Way to a Life of Complete Fulfilment.*
- **Watch:** Ann Masten's video *Ordinary Magic on the Developmental Road to Resilience.*

ALAN D. THOMPSON

Q:

Should I consider mentoring for my bright child?

A:

The highest performers always have a mentor that they can learn from.

Mentoring is another key ingredient of high performance. It's the fastest and most effective way of absorbing success—by learning about what it takes, and what didn't work.

American Supreme Court Justice Sonia Sotomayor knows all about the necessity of children having a role model or mentor. She says:

> *When a young person, even a gifted one, grows up without proximate living examples of what she may aspire to become— whether lawyer, scientist, artist, or leader in any realm—her goal remains abstract... But a role model in the flesh provides more than inspiration; his or her very existence is confirmation of possibilities...*

Adults have seen the proof that success comes from experience. Good news for bright children, this success doesn't have to come from their own experience. The most effective high performers chose to skip the learning through listening to the advice of someone who has been successful.

In my first book, *Best,* I wrote about the concept of mentoring for entrepreneurs:

> *Mentoring is the quickest and best way to get where you're going. Success comes from experience. The great thing is that it doesn't have to come from your own experience... You can skip the learning curve if you are open-minded enough to*

listen to the advice of someone who has been successful. In fact, there is no possible way to create success through just the intellect, or even just "feeling your way there". Success already exists in the minds of people who have been there before— seek their guidance! Life is too short to take the time to learn everything by trial and error when there are experts who are ready to help you.

One of the most effective, powerful and visible mentors of the last century was Dorothy Delay (who we met earlier). She was a high performer herself. Dorothy was a student when she participated in the accuracy check of one of the earliest versions of Stanford-Binet IQ tests—her result was an IQ of 180.

But she was most famous for her role in mentoring some of the greatest violinists of today. While teaching at Juilliard, she mentored notable players including Itzhak Perlman, Sarah Chang, Nadja Salerno-Sonnenberg, and Midori.

As a mentor, Dorothy Delay was obviously both gifted and talented (bright and brilliant). Importantly, she was also very patient. Many of her students have commented on her kindness and gentle way of being.

In her biography *Teaching Genius: Dorothy Delay and the Making of a Musician*, she is quoted as saying:

> *I found myself being interested in how certain talents can be developed because I have always had the desire to believe that environment is more important than heredity. So I said to myself, if somebody doesn't play in tune, it is because he hasn't learned how. Mr Galamian would say, "Oh, he has no ear. Don't waste your time." I would say to myself, I want to find out if I can get this person to play in tune, and I would experiment with all kinds of things, and Mr Galamian would say, "You don't have time for that," and I would think, Yes, but I want to know, and I would go on trying.*

Effective mentors *want* to draw out the child's best. They are invested in the child's success, and allow the child to discover it for themselves.

Find a mentor that is a good match for your child's temperament and attitude.

With very few exceptions—and none that I have experienced—mentors are always present early on in the lives of high performers.

Take it further

Questions for adults
- Who would you say were your mentors? What are you grateful for about them?
- What—or who—was present at the moment that you felt successful in life?
- What would you most like your child to learn?

Questions for children
- Who is the most interesting person you've ever met?
- What would it take to be more like them?

Resources
- **Read (with your child):** Dan Millman's book *Secret of the Peaceful Warrior: A Story About Courage and Love.*
- **Read:** Sonia Sotomayor's book *My Beloved World.*

Q:

My child loves playing with technology. How much technology is okay?

A:

The world is integrating technology rapidly. Bright children need to be given access to as much of this as possible, while remembering that being human always comes first.

Technology is improving humanity for the better, and it can be a vital ingredient of high performance. Bright children will (and do) harness and leverage technology in ways we can't yet comprehend. They also need to remember the importance of being human.

The chairman of Australian Mensa travels around the world participating in conferences and meetups. She told me about a humorous twist on the small talk that happens with new introductions at Mensa gatherings. In place of the cliché "So, what do you do?", this group of high IQ individuals were instead introducing themselves to each other by asking: "So, which branch of IT do you work in?"!

Technology is a given in today's world. Without question, personal use of technology will only increase, as the world embraces smart homes, smart cars, virtual reality, and artificial intelligence.

Each of these things improves our ability to use our capacity as humans. Researchers like American futurist Ray Kurzweil are doing their best to ensure that these are brought to us sooner rather than later. At the same time, others concerned with our "humanness" are working to ensure that we retain it, by prioritising real human relationships and interactions. This understanding can be enforced at home.

The late Steve Jobs, American technology entrepreneur (and CEO of Apple), was also a parent of four children. Interestingly, Steve and his wife minimised access to technology, in favour of real interaction. In an interview with *The New York Times* in 2014, Steve commented on his children and the new iPad: "They haven't used it. We limit how much technology our kids use at home."

Instead, Steve would discuss books and history with them during dinner, taking the time to foster real relationships. Devices were not welcome at the dinner table.

Plentiful research exists about children being addicted to screens, investing significant time every week staring at smart phones, tablets, computers, and televisions. However, that screen time can be used constructively.

Even though technology is increasing at an exponential rate (and it wouldn't be useful listing current tech as we advance so quickly!) here are some general practical applications.

Provide access to the world's knowledge as soon as appropriate. We live in an amazing time, with access to crowd-sourced and peer-reviewed answers to every conceivable question. Resources like *Wikipedia for Kids* (as a modern encyclopaedia), or *Khan Academy* (as a modern classroom at home) provide bright children with solutions to satisfy their "hunger to learn".

Consider basing your child's readiness on their actions, with supervision for young children. Provide them with access to uncover answers to their questions as soon as they are mentally and emotionally prepared.

Show children how to filter relevant information.

As the world is exposed to more and more data, it is increasingly easy to get "drunk on information". Being able to select high-quality information (without becoming overwhelmed by too much irrelevant data) is an important skill.

Bright children should be guided in ways to filter incoming information, whether it comes via an online search, choice of reading material, or exposure to emerging sources of input—including augmented and virtual reality.

Demonstrate the power of social interactions online. When age-appropriate, technology can be used to find and deepen connections between children on similar wavelengths. This is not just for children in isolated cities or towns; finding a mental equal can be a challenge even in the most populous places! Educational games like Second Life and Minecraft provide rich environments for bright children to discover that they are not alone, and to share experiences with peers around the world.

I believe that technology will only increase as a positive effect on the lives of bright children. However, like Steve Jobs, I prioritise real-life interactions.

Take it further

Questions for adults
- How have you used technology to improve your life?
- How is technology improving your child's life?

Questions for children
- How many friends do you have?
- How many of them are real-life friends, and how many of them are on your device?

Resources
- **Learn:** find answers using *Wikipedia for Kids – The Safe Filtered Wiki for Kids* at *www.wikiforkids.ws*.
- **Learn:** use the free online platform for learning at *www.khanacademy.org*.
- **Read:** Ray Kurzweil's book *How to Create a Mind: The Secret of Human Thought Revealed.*

Q:

What is coaching, and how can it help my child?

A:

Coaching is a process for uncovering your child's unique brilliance.

If your child needs IQ testing,
see a psychologist.

If your child is sick,
see a paediatrician.

If your child is ready to be brilliant,
see a coach.

Coaching for bright children is a very new field. All my coaching is with bright *families,* not bright children.

Every member of a family—parents, siblings, grandparents—is vitally important in a bright child's life. So I look for holistic results in the entire living environment—especially with those people closest to them. They are an integral part of a bright child's early years. The coaching focus is never just on the child. Instead, it is on the entire family unit. Children don't exist in isolation. Children are a product of their environment.

I remember one of my very first bright family coaching clients vividly—not so much because of the child, but because of the parent. The family had asked me to provide coaching for their son, Adam, because of his behavioural issues at home.

You see, Adam had a habit of beginning projects, getting most of the way through, and then quitting. In his mother's words: "He always stops just before he finishes." It didn't matter whether it was a test (he frequently just stopped when he didn't feel like answering any more), a puzzle (he often gave up before the end), or even a conversation. In fact, during the coaching session, Adam got up and walked out of the room, only to be called back by his mother. This happened several times.

I needed to understand what was happening here, so I pulled out a box of Lego...

If you've ever attended one of my seminars, or had coaching through Life Architect, you'll know about the Lego models. Clients build the answer to a coaching question using a small box of mixed Lego blocks.

The results are astounding. They always prove the quote (misattributed to Plato): "You can learn more about a person in an hour of play than in a year of conversation."

The Lego tool I use in coaching is derived from a consulting process created by professors Johan Roos and Bart Victor. That process, Lego Serious Play, is intended for corporations. It is used by the majority of the big players, including Google, Qantas, Shell, and Tupperware.

My version is slightly different, but looks at the same thing: results.

First, what does the individual construct? People learn best when building something external to themselves. A sand castle, a computer program, a painting.

Second, what can the individual imagine? When we "think through our fingers" we release creative energies, modes of thought, and ways of seeing things that may otherwise never be tapped. It is an inspiring process to witness, whether this imaginative release is from a CEO or from a five-year-old child. Sometimes there isn't much difference between the two.

It was during the Lego component of Adam's first

session that things took an interesting turn. Adam built a colourful model of a flourishing garden. His garden contained symbols that were meaningful to him, and he gave a solid explanation of how it all fitted together.

Adam's mother also built a colourful model. It was a large home, complete with multiple levels, a gazebo, and a water feature. But it was her explanation that gave me a deep insight into her son's behavioural issues.

Coach: I love your model! Tell me about what you've built.

Parent: It's a retirement home.

Coach: Really? Tell me more.

Parent: Well, I'm getting older now, and I want to stop working, settle down and retire.

Coach: *(Realising that Adam's mother is only in her early forties.)* But you're still young; you've got your whole life to live! What is it about retirement?

Parent: I've just had enough. I just want to retire...

Here was a living example of the process in

developmental psychology called "modelling". Adam was certainly imitating his mother's behaviour and attitudes. With very predictable results!

You don't have to read through all the research papers on modelling, because you'll see it in your own child.

> Does your child use eye contact?
> Do you use eye contact with your child?
>
> Does your child use positive language?
> Do you use positive language with your child?
>
> Does your child use good manners?
> Do you use good manners with your child?
>
> Does your child enjoy real conversation?
> Do you enjoy real conversation with your child?

While it's expected that our children will model the skills and disciplines of their mentors, it's equally true that children—especially bright children—model everything around them. So it follows that the things they are around the most will be picked up the most. It's called "being human"!

These "things" children pick up really can be *any* thing. General things like attitudes, perspectives, judgments, work ethic. Specific things like eating habits, language articulation, anger management, and relationships with others, including grandparents.

Of course, bright children are especially sensitive to the outside world, and model these things at a high rate.

Coaching for bright children and their families isn't about trying to teach something. It's not about convincing them of anything. It's not even about providing advice or mentoring them.

This is because, while adults nearly always *want* coaching (in the true sense of the word, they choose it), children are different. They have a different agenda. They want to run outside, build things, break them apart, and put them back together again.

So, coaching for bright children should be approached in a "kid-friendly" way.

My job as a coach is often simple—but not easy! With a range of proven tools from the most progressive countries, choosing which tools to apply based on the individual and their current state is both an art and a science. A six-year-old gifted child can express their fears—and dreams—using our customised version of Lego Serious Play. A bright 10-year-old girl with shaky confidence can learn a different way of looking at herself using the Gallup StrengthsExplorer assessment. A 16-year-old boy seeking to understand himself and his family and peers can benefit from a family version of a well-researched behavioural profiling tool. And of course, the sensitive and specific questioning and tone of a coach can encourage bright children to explore new ways of thinking more widely.

These are the same types of questions and tools used for coaching entrepreneurs and executives, just adapted for children.

In my own coaching practice, I always have specific questions that I ask bright families to make sure we would be a good fit. Questions can make people *think*, which is sometimes rare! If they are well-crafted questions, they let the family experience the power of coaching conversations. Note that I didn't say coaching *advice*.

In the coaching room, my first question to new children is nearly always: **What are five things you are good at?** This starts the conversation out on the right wavelength. We're here to explore and uncover, not to undergo therapy! It also begins our dialogue by empowering the child to participate and challenge themselves to come up with some real answers.

My next question might be: **What are five words that describe you?**

(It's useful for you to answer these questions as well. I've seen the results of these across a wide range of ages, cultures, and people. They work. They change perspectives for the better.)

These questions allow the child to explore more

than one option—five, in fact! I can always tell when the child is either supremely confident in who they are (and rattle off a longer list) or pushing to think of the next thing (sometimes while looking at their parents for approval).

Next I might want to know: **On a scale from 1 to 10, how much do you like school?** or **On a scale from 1 to 10, how much do you like your teacher?**

I love this one, as it provides real metrics and measurements for where they *think* they are. And that's all that matters—how *are* they? No, really, *how are they right now?*

The focus on the school environment, above even the home environment, is there for a reason. A typical day in the life of a bright child, especially with the demands of sleep on a heavily taxed central processing unit (or brain) is divided to give school the foremost weighting. In fact, it usually looks a bit like this:

Activity	Hours	%
Sleep	12	50
School	7	30
Home	5	20

Of course, the answers are even more powerful if the child is home-schooled. I might then expand on this with: **What specifically do you like about your teacher?** Depending on the age group, there might be a flowery explanation of all the things they like and appreciate about their teacher. This emotional connection is important for the family to see. A child learns through their sense of relationship to the subject.

To further investigate their relationships, I ask: **How many friends do you have?** In this modern world, perhaps needing to add: **How many of them are close, how many of them are just online friends?**

Looking into the family dynamic is a major part of the coaching process. But it helps to get a feel for what the child thinks. So: **How do you get along with your brother or sister?**

How about this one: **What's your biggest challenge at school?** Notice in this question I don't ask anything vague or wishy-washy. Bright children are our future. I want to know what's holding them back—the same type of question I would ask an executive or billionaire entrepreneur.

These questions don't need to come in any rigid linear sequence. I use more than the ones detailed above. I mix them up. I sometimes leave them out, and ask new questions in the moment. Coaching sessions are a creation, so the more creativity we bring into it—especially with our creative children!—the more effective we will be.

When coaching bright families, I try to remember the child's perspective in interacting with a new person:

My degrees are not important to them.

My credentials are not important to them.

How many papers I've written is not important to them.

How many countries I've worked in is not important to them.

My knowledge of industry buzzwords is **definitely** not important to them.

In fact, all of those things can get in the way of an authentic conversation, and a real coaching relationship…

A child only cares about one thing. And that is the same thing that adults care about:

How can I help them in this moment?

Take it further

Questions for adults
- If you could ask your child anything, what would it be?
- If you could give your child anything, what would it be?

Questions for children
- What would it feel like to always know the best answer?
- What do you think causes you to do so well?
- How could you improve?

Resources
- **Read:** Judy Rees and Wendy Sullivan's book *Clean Language: Revealing Metaphors and Opening Minds.*

ALAN D. THOMPSON

Part 3: Tips for raising brilliance

Bright children only have one thing in common—an advanced brain. All the rest is new, different, and evolving in the child you have in front of you.

That means that these tips cannot be applied to all bright children, all of the time. Some of them may work for you; some of them may not. Discover the individual differences in your bright child.

These individual differences include temperament, personality, attitude, behaviour, chronological age, mental age, and everything in between.

Remember that bright children can't be hot-housed. This applies to brilliance as well. As we've seen, there is a "self-steering" component to high performers. Yes, they need to be identified and encouraged. But they alone have the responsibility to make the choice to internalise the commitment to produce the effort to define the outcome to reveal brilliance!

Brightness is not enough to produce brilliance. Superstars come from a combination of the key ingredients I've provided, and something else. Perhaps like the notion that "one and one makes three", brilliance requires a certain magic.

Fortunately, that magic is visible—for those who look for it.

Seeing superstars, listening to their worlds, and moving out of the way can be distilled into these tips.

1. **Practice extreme self care.** We've seen how powerful modelling is in the lives of bright children. Bright children become bright adults, so give them your best self.

2. **Give your child absolute support and acceptance.** This doesn't mean that you have to like their behaviour all the time. Accept them for who they are, not their capacity or potential.

3. **Let them know that they are powerful.** Show your child that they are powerful enough to create something important.

4. **Respect the individuality and uniqueness of every bright child.** This means that what worked for one may not be the same thing that works for another.

5. **Provide opportunities to make decisions.** Let them make choices and learn from experience.

6. **Demonstrate deep breathing (also called belly or diaphragmatic breathing).** Allow bright children to relax their central nervous system and reduce stress.

7. **Ask as many questions as they ask you!** Let them discover solutions using their own problem-solving skills and available resources.

8. **Ensure your child can see the big picture.** High performers can change the world. Let them know it.

9. **Minimise rules.** Boundaries are important, but not if they stifle creativity and growth.

10. **Teach financial literacy early.** Start with giving responsibility during shopping trips.

11. **Get them involved with their interests.** Find peers, events, competitions, and resources to help them become involved with the world.

12. **Show optimism.** Share positive stories and inspirational talks with your child.

13. **Get involved with teachers.** Bright children spend the majority of their waking hours learning. Ensure that it is effective.

14. **Stay connected.** Be aware of any issues or challenges that appear in your child's life.

15. **Minimise TV watching.** Consuming information is only one part of the equation. Bright children love creating!

16. **Teach bright children how to talk back to a worried mind.** Telling an anxious mind "stop, this is okay" is an effective way for bright children to take control of themselves.

17. **Respect struggle in the learning process.** Resist the temptation to give an answer or show how to solve a problem. Let them wrestle with a problem; that's what learning is about.

18. **Let them fail!** Do not rush in to save your child when they make a mistake. Both home and school should be safe places in which to learn to deal with mistakes.

19. **Allow independent learning.** Let bright children create their own learning paths and learn by doing.

20. **Model confidence.** Research has found that the foundation of a bright child's confidence is established by the age of five. But it is built every day!

21. **Integrate movement.** Bright children love to move, their bodies are used as a way to express what's going on in their brains.

22. **Create positive environments.** Increase your home "positivity ratio" using more supportive language.

23. **Don't catastrophise negative emotions: listen to them.** Demonstrate self-acceptance by listening to a child's anger or sadness.

24. **Limit homework, testing, and forced extra-curricular activities.** Avoid overwhelming and stifling curiosity. Aim for quality, not quantity.

25. **Don't bring anger into discipline.** If you feel yourself getting angry, leave the situation until you have reset. Sensitive children will be adversely affected by angry discipline.

26. **Be open with "age-appropriate" everything, including the human body.** And remember, "age-appropriate" doesn't mean chronological age as much as mental age.

27. **Share successes.** Allow the whole family to celebrate successes.

28. **Allow time to recover after setbacks.** Bright children need time to regroup after a failure—physical, mental, or emotional.

29. **Encourage "thinking big".** Find ways for your child to realise their strengths and talents.

30. **Introduce negotiation early.** Help your bright child design and adopt strategies for getting what they want.

31. **Let them play.** When children play, they engage all of their creative energies. This can be physical play, electronic game play, or even playing with work!

32. **Encourage reading stories about successful people.** Allow them to see the whole story behind high performance and what it takes to be bold.

33. **Introduce them to new languages.** Bright children communicate in a number of different ways, and usually learn rapidly. Suggest or let them choose a new language.

34. **Lead by example.** Model brilliance.

35. **Encourage the discovery of music.** There is a correlation between brightness and appreciation of music.

36. **Address behaviour.** Point out what is wrong with the behaviour, not the child.

37. **Give chores.** There is ongoing research into the positive results of having responsibility from a young age.

38. **Ensure that they are eating healthy food.** Advanced brains need quality fuel, frequently.

39. **Encourage opinions.** Your child has responses to everything going on around them. Let them express this as opinions.

40. **Teach thinking, not just memorisation.** Sure, memorisation is important. But critical thinking (including creative problem solving) is becoming more valuable.

41. **Share your own mistakes.** It is important for bright children to see how you make mistakes, fail, and overcome adversity.

42. **Encourage reading.** There is a multitude of research on the long-term benefits of reading for young children.

43. **Encourage your bright child to use a journal.** Pouring thoughts onto the page often frees up space on the mental hard drive!

44. **Cultivate gratitude.** Practise expressing frequent gratitude by talking about things you are thankful for, and ask the same of your child. This can be a nightly exercise before sleep.

45. **Teach early maths skills.** Research has found that mastery of early maths skills predicts future maths achievement—and also future reading achievement!

46. **Recall past achievements.** Teach your child that they are able to get better and better by recalling ways they have previously succeeded—or failed and overcome.

47. **Show how to turn a challenge into an opportunity.** Show your bright child how to cope with negative experiences including rejection.

48. **Catch a child doing something right.** This can be something as simple as expressing appreciation for your child's questions and observations.

49. **Show the importance of kindness.** Do we really need another mean celebrity or arrogant CEO?

50. **Encourage focus.** Being able to focus on one goal or project is important.

51. **Acknowledge, don't praise**. Research has found that children whose parents overvalued them at an early age were more likely to be narcissists later on.

52. **Discuss feelings.** The other side of logic and thinking: feelings and emotions are important for a bright child to be able to identify and talk about.

53. **Provide content that is just ahead of your child's level of cognitive development.** Not too easy to lack challenge, but not too hard to be frustrating.

54. **Allow imagination.** Albert Einstein's famous quote is everywhere: "Imagination is more important than knowledge." Allow it.

55. **Be consistent.** Bright children usually have prodigious memories. If you say that you are going to do something, then do it. This includes discipline. If they are misbehaving, follow through on previously agreed consequences.

56. **Use visual models.** Most bright children learn visually. Try mind mapping, graph paper, photos, diagrams, and other visual presentation methods for learning and exploring new content.

57. **Make room for social skills.** Researchers tracked more than 700 children from kindergarten to age 25, and found a link between their social skills as young children and their success as young adults two decades later.

58. **Keep a list of your child's big questions or problems to be solved.** They can use these later as prompts for projects or writing.

59. **Use colour-coding wherever practicable.** Highlighters, coloured pens, or just bursts of colour help link concepts in a bright child's mind.

60. **Teach healthy competition.** Encourage winning (and the feeling of exhilaration), but don't always let bright children win. Winning builds confidence; losing builds character.

61. **Encourage strong relationships.** This includes with adults, other children, and groups. Strong and supportive relationships are a key ingredient in high performance.

62. **Provide specific examples of your strengths.** It is important for bright children to see how you operate from your strengths.

63. **Stay on top of current research.** While most research won't go "out-of-date", researchers are publishing new findings all the time. Put down the out-of-date stuff and pick up the latest of the greatest.

64. **Understand individual communication styles.** Figure out or assess how your bright child is wired for communication, and embrace it.

65. **Stay hydrated!** The human brain needs water to function effectively.

66. **Initiate conversations about topics that improve their life.** It might be an interest, current events, or a success story.

67. **Ask open-ended questions.** These can be about simple, day-to-day tasks, giving your child the initiative to form answers and find solutions.

68. **Ensure they get enough sleep.** A number of studies prove that some behavioural issues stem from lack of sleep. Advanced brains need sleep.

69. **Minimise time-wasting distractions.** This starts with leading by example, including minimising unnecessary checking of phone and email.

70. **Encourage independence.** Allow bright children to create their own path early on.

71. **Know where to send them when they are stuck on a problem.** This means having an awareness of what is out there—such as online materials, books, and experts.

72. **Engage in your child's projects.** When appropriate, give support, show interest, and encourage them to use available resources.

73. **Demonstrate guided meditation.** Fantastic for creative children! Find a place to relax and meditate, tell a story for 20 minutes in a calm, measured way.

74. **Don't belittle your child.** Trying to undercut, remove ego, warn of "getting a big head", or other "tall poppy syndrome" attacks are counter-productive.

75. **Remember that you have responsibility—as the adult—to make adult decisions.** Bright children are still children, just with advanced brains. This means that where an adult has the wisdom and life experience they are responsible for finding the right path.

76. **Answer questions.** Support curiosity. Treat probing questions seriously and respectfully rather than undermining them.

77. **Link confidence to who they are, not what they achieve.** Achievement is not the goal. The goal is to be loved for who they are, not their capacity.

78. **Have fun with them.** Remember, because it can easily be forgotten, that bright children have an incredible sense of humour.

79. **Teach study skills.** Show children how to study. Include time management, task analysis and breakdown, planning, and prioritisation.

80. **Affirm positive parts of life.** During the day or before bed, read daily affirmations, or write them yourself.

81. **Consider IQ testing with a psychologist.** For bright children at the top, it can definitely be useful to have visible metrics.

82. **Teach children to develop and rely on their intuition.** That "gut feeling" is important to listen to and understand.

83. **Hold the best and highest view of your child's capacity.** Refuse to accept a child's negative self-concept.

84. **Show your bright child how to plan and schedule.** Use a calendar, a diary, or another way of looking to the future.

85. **Prompt your bright child to connect the dots between seemingly unrelated data.** Start at home, but bring in their hobbies and interests.

86. **Give your time.** It's one of the most valuable things to a bright child. Don't be "too busy": give them your self.

87. **Be slow to offer advice.** One of the cardinal rules of coaching, and applicable also to advanced parenting. Allow them to use their own wisdom.

88. **Express your acceptance non-verbally as well.** It is easy to offer verbal acceptance. Show them that you mean it through eye contact, a hug, or a touch on the arm.

89. **Focus on your child's strengths.** Consider strengths coaching to deeply understand and realise your child's specific talents.

90. **Don't pressure your bright child to fit in socially.** Many bright children feel different during adolescence. Help them to feel comfortable with their differences and redirect their energies towards positive activities.

91. **Create a calming physical space for them.** This can include every physical element: music (headphones), comfort (toys), self-expression (markers), and more.

92. **Try Dr Angela Duckworth's "hard thing rule" at home.** Every family member must be engaged in their own personal hard activity (one that takes more than six months to achieve), and provide regular feedback on progress.

93. **Design a personalised learning program with your child.** Leverage resources like *KhanAcademy.org* or *iTunes U.*

94. **Leave new books lying around the house.** Bright children love discovering things, not necessarily being told what to do!

95. **Name and identify the range of feelings and emotions.** It is helpful for a bright child to be able to name a particular feeling in the moment.

96. **Encourage memorisation strategies.** Memorisation gets a bad rap, but it is a core part of life, and bright children are at a distinct advantage. Use audio recordings, flash cards, repetition, mnemonics, and stories to embed necessary information.

97. **Let your own excitement shine through.** Bright children are always watching and listening; model a deeper passion for life.

98. **Explore multiple perspectives with your child.** Bring in different people's perspectives, different times and centuries, and even new physical perspectives (stand on the desk!).

99. **Discuss ethics.** While not often taught directly, understanding ethics is very powerful in living authentically.

100. **Learn from your child.** It's a two-way street, and bright children have a lot to offer.

ALAN D. THOMPSON

Epilogue

This is an exciting time to be alive! The capacities and potentialities of bright children are unlike anything I've seen before.

Remember that you are also fully supported and accepted. Online resources (many of them out of the United States, though that is changing rapidly), local mentors, trained professionals, and other parents are available to you. Find them, seek them out, and share with them.

You've got tremendous support on this well-trodden path.

ALAN D. THOMPSON

Other acknowledgments

In addition to my annual checkup with **Erin Pavlina, Slade Roberson** gave very specific guidance in our sessions together. You have both changed my life.

Andrea J. Lee walked by my side during this pioneering path of helping bright families reveal their brilliance. **Steve Hardison** has been providing me with insights since I first sat in his room in Mesa, Arizona, several years ago.

My colleagues in the psychology, counselling, and coaching fields gave selflessly in every conversation—often several hours at a time—as I continued to explore brightness and high performance in the 21st century. What a rush! **Otto Siegel** at Genius Coaching, **Michele Juratowitch** at Clearing Skies, **Karen King** at Brainbox, and **Gail Byrne** at Exceptional Children.

Thank you to all the staff at **Australian Mensa** for your support over the last decade, especially the various Gifted Children's Coordinators (past and present, national and state). Thank you to all the proactive parents, families, and young Mensans for everything you bring to the organisation.

Nat Caudle for your vibrancy and charisma in getting the word out. **Lincoln Justus**' sunshine burst through in the spectacularly bright cover—thank you!

The team! Now in our fifth year working together, I finally get to refer to **Jessie Cat** (Pencil Paws Consulting) as my "long-time" editor! Wonderful work. **Rob Ashton** pulled out all stops (and the Australian Macquarie dictionary) for me in his impeccable proofreading. Thanks also to advice from **Jim Heath** (Viacorp).

I am only able to bring these words to life—and the written page—when I feel the pull of inspiration. When I feel myself getting into this "zone", I always, *always* press the play button on visceral and earth-moving music. For *Bright*, this has included compositions from **Charlie Smalls (The Wiz)**, **Saverio Grandi & Gaetano Curreri (Stadio)**, **Rami Yacoub**, and **Gary Stadler.** There is a magic brought to the world through the physical translation of your work to others.

Thank you to **each and every one of my bright family clients, both parents and children**. Your individual belief in and support of yourselves is the driving force behind the biggest and most exciting expansion of humanity's capacity the world has ever seen.

About the author

Alan D. Thompson is a certified personal and professional coach, facilitator, and consultant. He has more than 15 years of international experience in multicultural environments in Australia, New Zealand, North America, China, and throughout Asia.

He is widely regarded as one of the world's foremost gifted coaches. He specialises in working with individual high-potential achievers, entrepreneurs, and gifted families, and is an expert on brilliant performance in the arena of life.

Alan studied Computer Science, including electives from the School of Psychology. In 1999, he created his first company, Imagine Unlimited.

Having spent more than a decade as a sound designer to high-performing celebrities, Alan was a part of the creative and technical teams behind some of the largest international events on the planet (Red Bull Air Race, Christmas at the Sydney Opera House, Taipei Dome). He has worked with many high-performing young stars, including the Australian Billy Elliot, Nikki Webster, and the cast of Andrew Lloyd Webber's *Cats* in Asia.

He is an Associate Certified Coach (ACC) with the International Coach Federation (ICF), working and training extensively throughout Singapore, Hong Kong, the United States, and China. He is also a Certified Genius Coach (USA).

Alan is the National Gifted Children's Coordinator for Australian Mensa.

Along with Professor Mark C. Williams, he is a founder of the Australia–Asia Positive Psychology Institute.

He is an engaging speaker, presenting gifted parent workshops throughout Asia, gifted teacher professional development seminars in Australia, and a new online program for gifted parents and teachers at:

LifeArchitect.tv.

Alan has published several works, including the books *Best: A practical guide to living your best life* and *Welcome: Stories to wake up to!*

Alan currently lives in Perth, Western Australia. For more information on Alan and his work, visit:

LifeArchitect.com.au

What Alan is up to

Speaking. Alan presents seminars and workshops at many state, national, and international conferences. He also runs programs for education, including teacher professional development. Each topic can be delivered as a stand-alone presentation, workshop (if appropriate), or a keynote address.

Writing. Alan continues to translate current research into digestible (and practical) tools for parents, educators, and professionals. His articles are made available to journals and reputable publications around the world.

Coaching. Family clients are extraordinary. One-on-one (or coach-and-family) sessions continue to be delivered in-person for local and travelling clients. Skype, video call and in-person sessions are available for interstate and international clients.

ALAN D. THOMPSON

Next steps...

Bright families are exhilarating! My current research and coaching focuses on bright children who are ready either to move into, or move more deeply into, brilliance. Musical prodigies. Sports stars. Academic high performers. Chess players. Maths wizards. Children with increasingly high capacities, and the willingness to learn more about themselves (especially their own brains) to give them an early start on brilliance.

Bright children have the natural building blocks to help our planet evolve further: deep curiosity, rapid processing, extreme creativity, broad information retention, abstract comprehension, and absolute independence.

To be their best, they need a healthy environment, the right set of tools, a positive mental attitude, to be raised in an inspiring community, in an evolving culture, with sincere encouragement, and customised learning (without so much focus on teaching).

Bright children are primed for performance. They learn rapidly and intensely! They need effective tools to understand themselves and function in the world—as early as possible. Supported by their parents, families, and choice of education, we integrate new coaching tools to identify your child's strengths and ideal growth environment.

Bright children are everywhere! My family clients come from all walks of life; there is no fixed nationality or demographic. Our work together is always effective.

If you have a bright child who is ready to move into their own brilliance and live to their full capacity, or if you are simply interested in learning more about my work, please contact me directly:

alan@LifeArchitect.com.au

Made in the USA
Las Vegas, NV
26 February 2024